Pastor Tricia
You are a powerful!
Lioness in the L
You are anointed?
The Nations! The B___! You
Days are before you! You
A blessing and a joy to my life
A wonderful spiritual daughter!

ANOINTED TO ROAR
By: Dr. Brian Alton
© 2013-Desert Rose Community Church

Love
Dr. Brian Alton
2014

GATEWAY PRESS
A Division of Aion Group Multimedia
and Gateway International Bible Institute

Chapter 1
The Lion Hath Roared!

The lion has forever been a symbol of strength, power and ferocity. Seeing the majestic species up-close is sure to be a spine-tingling experience. African lions are the most social of all big cats and live together in groups, or *prides*. A *pride* consists of about 12 lions. The male lions defend the pride's territory while females do most of the hunting. Despite this, the males always eat first. A lion's roar can be heard from as far as five miles away. A lion can run 50 mph (for short distances), and leap as far as 36 feet. A good gauge of a male lion's age is the darkness of his mane; the darker the mane, the older the lion. Even though the lion is sometimes referred to as the "King of the Jungle", it actually likes to live in grasslands and plains.

In the Biblical study of the word *lion,* we discover there are nine different ways the word is translated in the Hebrew language. Although I have listed them in this teaching material, we will not attempt an in-depth exegesis on the usage of the word. The Bible is filled with code words hidden in various parts of the scripture-without an explanation for their presence, until the exact time the Holy Spirit wishes to reveal the hidden meaning of either their interpretation or location. With that noted, I would encourage all of you avid readers and students of the Scriptures who like in-depth study and research to locate the usage of the name "lion" in the many passages of scripture throughout the Bible. Their usage gives special clarity and authority to my claim that the gift of prophecy is like "a roaring lion". These nine names are hidden from the average reader because most people do not have the time to look up the meaning of names, people, cities, nations etc., but to those who are willing to dive deeper into the layers of the Word of God, they will discover far greater and exceeding revelations than they have ever known before.

The following come from names in the Genealogy of Christ, reflecting the various elements of Christ's prophetic gifting and anointing:

The Lion	
Arieh	2 Kings 15:25
My God Is A Lion	
Areli	Genesis 46:16
The Lion Is Enough	
Aridai	Esther 9:9
The Lion Of The Decree	
Aridatha	Esther 9:8
The Lion's Den	
Argob	Deut. 3:4
The Son Of God Is Lion-Like	
Arioch	Genesis 46:6
The Lion Of Perpetual Rejoicing	
Arnaho	1 Chr. 3:21
The Lion of God Is A Light At the Altar	
Ariel	Ezra, 8:16
My Position In God Is Like Unto a Lion Who Roars from its Den	
Arlsaiahi	Esther, 9:9

The fact that there is a special anointing for a special ministry is no secret. This anointing often comes into our lives even before our birth, just as John the Baptist was filled with the Holy Spirit while still yet in his mother's womb. From Genesis 3 to Matthew 3, the promise of the coming Christ was continually held before the nation of Israel as the hope of the world. The Holy One, The

Anointed One, came in due time just as was predicted by the roaring prophets of old. While millions waited for the Kings appearing and said the Messiah will come in this manner or in that manner, John the Baptist declared (or rather, John roared), "He is coming! When the Promised One comes He will baptize you with the Holy Ghost and fire!"

"I indeed baptize you with water unto repentance, but He who is coming after me is mightier than I, whose sandals I am not worthy to carry. He will baptize you with the Holy Spirit and fire." (Matt. 3:11 NKJV)

The Prophet Amos wrote, "The lion hath roared, who will not fear? The Lord God hath spoken, who can but prophesy?" (Amos 3:8 KJV). In this passage, the prophet is saying that the lion's roar of the scriptures is not heard in the downbeat of defeat, but in the upbeat of victory. As the lion lives in the jungle without fear of other natural predators, so shall the believer live in the Spirit, in this world, walking in peace throughout their natural lives, having no fear and roaring in victory over every spiritual predator sent by the enemy.

"You shall seek them and not find them; those who contended with you. Those who war against you shall be as nothing, as a nonexistent thing. For I, the Lord your God, will hold your right hand, saying to you, 'Fear not, I will help you.'" (Isa. 41:12-13 NKJV)

There is a revelatory key that can open up one of the greatest truths you have ever known. This key is the three prophetic revelations concerning the Lion of the tribe of Judah. The Lion of Judah is the single greatest source of power available to the believer.

The first revelation is found within the tribe of Judah. The Judah tribe is the most praising people among all the twelve tribes. Secondly, the lion is the message giver on Judah's banner, which is the standard of the tribe of Judah. The standard with the lion on it, is the banner that they carried into every battle. Lastly, it is also the banner displayed as the priests carried the Ark of the Covenant on their shoulders across the Jordan River. Yes- *Judah* means "praise" or "to praise". The word is first used in the Old Testament (O.T.) Genesis 29:35, "Leah conceived again, and when she gave birth to a son she said, 'This time I will praise the Lord.' So she named him Judah..." It is pronounced *Ye-hu-dah*. The word *Jew* comes from *Judah*. The three tribes remaining after the golden calf debacle in the wilderness were Levi, Benjamin, and Judah- collectively called "the Jews"; those left to praise God on earth. Therefore, the Judah tribe is the praising tribe. It was from the tribe of Judah that Jesus Christ and King David sprang. In the book of Judges, we see two instances where the Lord said the tribe of Judah is to go up first against their enemies in battle. The first occurrence is found in Judges 1:2, following the death of Joshua. When the children of Israel inquired of the Lord, "Who should go up first against the Canaanites?", The Lord responded, "Judah shall go up..." The second is found in Judges 20:18, when once again the children of Israel inquired of the Lord who was to go up first against the sons of Benjamin. Again, the Lord's answer to them was, "Judah shall go up first". While Judges, Chapters 1 and 20 tell of battle in the human realm where the praise tribe went out first against their enemies, we must ask ourselves a question: When we find ourselves doing battle in the spirit realm, what or who goes first before us in battle? Do we enter the battle alone, or do we allow Judah (or praise) to go first? The Word of God says that flesh and spirit are constantly at war with one another (Gal. 5:17). Praise is not an act of the flesh; it is an attitude of the heart. It takes discipline to train our spirits to send out praise as we enter a battle with our enemy, the devil.

David chose to live and govern his own life and kingdom with a life of praise. In Psalm 34, we see how David made a conscious decision to bless (to praise) the Lord at all times. He chose to continually keep the praises of God in his mouth. This means that he daily made a choice to live in the upbeat of praise and victory instead of the downbeat of fear and defeat. Praising God when we see no logical reason to do so gives us power to face every obstacle. Praise changes our focus and shifts our minds off the problem and onto God's power to sustain us. In our sacrificial praise, God may choose, in His sovereignty, to change us before He brings change to the situation. Because King Jehoshaphat stationed a praise choir to march before the army in 2 Chronicles 20, by the hand of God, there was no battle to be fought when they reached the battleground. The enemies of God's people destroyed themselves.

I want to challenge those of you who may be neck-deep in battle right now; in the heat of our spiritual battle let Judah go up first. Let the praises of God go forth out of your mouth. Let the praises of God be as rivers of living water flowing from your belly (John 7:38). Before you spend hours just talking about the problem and how bad things are, stir up the power that God has already given you in your praise to Him; sacrificial though it may be. This is the kind of praise that reaches the heart of God. It is this kind of faith-building praise that will sustain you while you wait on God. This is the kind of praise that will keep you focused on God's promise, His plan, and His provision; it will keep you grounded in His faithfulness, and determined to press into your blessing!

ANOINTED TO ROAR

The three prophetic revelations of the Lion of the tribe of Judah sound like such simple truths, so how could they possibly open up one of the greatest truths I have ever known? Well, I am so glad you asked this question. You see, prophetically this means that "the Lion" led them out of their wilderness and into their promised land. He led them out that He might bring them into the mountain of His inheritance. The appearance of the lion speaks of strength and courage, which is the power that enables the worshipper (the Judah tribe) to ascend the mountain of praise during their journey into possessing their land of promise!

The Face of the Lion

Once Israel was in the Promised Land, the face of a lion was engraved in several places in the tabernacle and in the temple. "And it was made with cherubim and palm trees, so that a palm tree was between a cherub and a cherub; and every cherub had two faces; so that the face of a man was toward the palm tree on the one side, and the face of a young lion toward the palm tree on the other side: it was made through all the house round about." (Ez. 41:18-19).

Prophetically speaking, the most important symbol in this passage is the face of the lion. Symbolically, the lion represents a king. The lion is thought of as a ruler in the animal kingdom. The lion represents the kingly anointing in the same way the ox represents the burden carrier. Here in Ezekiel 41:18-19, we see the meaning of "plumb and balance". The lion's anointing shows both power and humility in the four faces of the cherubim, but the picture here is that of a *young* lion. The young lion is known for its agility and it's being happy and joyful romping about the pride. A mature lion is known to be ferocious in battle. An old lion is known for its cleverness and wisdom and its ability to catch younger, smaller prey with ease. Thus, the lion's anointing supports us, informs us, empowers us, and carries us as if on a great tidal wave.

The Holy Spirit manifests Christ's nature in what we call "the anointing". According to Isaiah 10:27, "It shall come to pass in that day that his burden will be taken away from your shoulder, and his yoke from your neck and the yoke will be destroyed because of the anointing oil." 1 John 2:27 says, "But the anointing which you have received from Him abides in you, and you do not need that anyone teach you; but as the same anointing teaches you concerning all things, and is true, and is not a lie, and just as it has taught you, you will abide in Him." With this anointing, the believer is as well equipped to live in the midst of the dangers of this present age, just as a lion is well equipped to live in the deep dark jungle.

In Ezekiel 41, we also see the picture of a cherub. The first time a cherub is mentioned in scripture was in reference to Lucifer. I do not want to give too much teaching to the account of this fallen cherub now named Satan; the arch nemeses of Christ, His chosen people and His Church. However, it is very important to grasp a few important scriptural truths to better help us understand how the Lion of Heaven, Jesus our Messiah is, was, and forever will be The Master – the "Lion King" over His heavenly domain.

Seraphim and Cherubim are angelic imageries in sacred scripture with hidden mysteries. They are two heavenly beings with wings who are often associated with the Presence of God, especially around His Throne (Isa. 6:2-6; Ex. 25:20-22; Ez. 1:4-28; 10:1-22; Rev. 4:5-9). Both heavenly beings are fiery, burning spirits as described in their Hebrew definition "*saraph*" and "*kerub*." The words *cherub* and *cherubim* occur about a hundred times in the Bible, but descriptive imagery of Cherubim is scarce. Cherubim are often referred to as members of "the second order of angels" or "celestial beings". They are considered Guarding Angels of Light.

In Ezekiel 28, the roaring prophet Ezekiel was speaking of Satan as he directed his prophetic words at the prince of Tyre. Satan was the former anointed guarding cherub named Lucifer who had once possessed great authority and moved and walked among all the other angelic principalities and powers on the Holy mountain of God in the midst of the fiery stones (Ez. 28:14). This gives us great explanation in 2 Corinthians 11:14 as to how Satan has the ability to transform himself into an angel of light.

"For such are false apostles, deceitful workers, transforming themselves into apostles of Christ. And no wonder! For Satan himself transforms himself into an angel of light. Therefore, it is no great thing if his ministers also transform themselves into ministers of righteousness, whose end will be according to their works." (2 Cor. 11:13-15)

Isaiah 14, reveals that Lucifer was the first chief worshipping cherub and he became, through self-worship, the one who "fell like lightning from heaven" and became known as the Devil (Luke 10:18). Satan fell because of pride. He desired to be God, not a servant of God.

Notice the many "I will..." statements found in Isaiah 14:12-15, "How you are fallen from heaven, O Lucifer, son of the morning! How you are cut down to the ground, You who weakened the nations! For you have said in your heart: 'I will ascend into heaven, I will exalt my throne above the stars of God; I will also sit on the mount of the congregation on the farthest sides of the north; I will ascend above the heights of the clouds, I will be like the Most High.' Yet you shall be brought down to Sheol, to the lowest depths of the Pit."

Ezekiel 28:12-19, describes Satan as an exceedingly beautiful angel. "You were the seal of perfection, full of wisdom and perfect in beauty. You were in Eden, the garden of God; every precious stone was your covering: The sardius, topaz, and diamond, beryl, onyx, and jasper, sapphire, turquoise, and emerald with gold. The workmanship of your timbrels and pipes was prepared for you on the day you were created. You were the anointed cherub who covers; I established you; you were on the holy mountain of God; you walked back and forth in the midst of fiery stones. You were perfect in your ways from the day you were created, till iniquity was found in you. By the abundance of your trading, you became filled with violence within, and you sinned; Therefore I cast you as a profane thing out of the mountain of God, and I destroyed you, O covering cherub, from the midst of the fiery stones. Your heart was lifted up because of your beauty; you corrupted your wisdom for the sake of your splendor; I cast you to the ground, I laid you before kings that they might gaze at you. You defiled your sanctuaries by the multitude of your iniquities, by the iniquity of your trading; therefore I brought fire from your midst; it devoured you, and I turned you to ashes upon the earth in the sight of all who saw you. All who knew you among the peoples are astonished at you; you have become a horror, and shall be no more forever."

Satan was likely the highest of all cherubs, the most beautiful of all of God's angelic creations, but he was not content in his beauty and elevated position. Instead, Satan desired to BE God, to essentially kick God off His throne of praise and take over the rule of the universe. Satan didn't just desire all the praise of God, but he desired to be THE God, and interestingly enough, that is what Satan tempted Adam and Eve within the Garden of Eden (see Gen. 3:1-5). Genesis 3:2-4 states, "And the woman said to the serpent, 'We may eat the fruit of the trees of the garden; but of the fruit of the tree which is in the midst of the garden, God has said, 'You shall not eat it, nor shall you touch it, lest you die.'" Then the serpent said to the woman, "You will not surely die. For God knows that in the day you eat of it your eyes will be opened, and you will be like God, knowing good and evil."

How great was Satan's fall from Heaven? We see two passages that describe this event in better detail:

Revelation 12:3-4 NKJV: "And another sign appeared in heaven: behold, a great, fiery red dragon having seven heads and ten horns, and seven diadems on his heads. His tail drew a third of the stars of heaven and threw them to the earth."

Luke 10:17-18, NKJV: "Then the seventy returned with joy, saying, 'Lord, even the demons are subject to us in Your name.'" And He said to them, "I saw Satan fall like lightning from heaven."

I would like to note here that the word *fall* in Luke 10:18 is not an accurate description in this particular passage. It would be far more accurate to say that God "cast Satan out" of Heaven (Isa. 14:15; Ez. 28:16-17). But here in Luke 10, Jesus was referring to the spiritual conflict that took place in heaven and refers to Satan's initial fall from heavenly perfection and being "cast out" from heaven.

Seventy Young Lions Sent

In Luke 10:1 Jesus, The Lion of Judah appointed and sent out 70 young, inexperienced lions from His pride (the 70 disciples) into the countryside of Israel to go and learn how to be like Him; roaring prophetic lions that are able to walk in the Lion's Anointing and power in order to take authority and dominion to be masters over their cities, and their jungles filled with evil predators called the world and the devil.

"After these things the Lord appointed seventy others also, and sent them two by two before His face into every city and place where He Himself was about to go." (Luke 10:1)

"Then the seventy returned with joy, saying, 'Lord, even the demons are subject to us in Your name.'" (Luke 10:17)

"Behold, I give you the authority to trample on serpents and scorpions, and over all the power of the enemy, and nothing shall by any means hurt you." (Luke 10:19)

These 70 disciples rose up in the Lion's Anointing and began to roar throughout the cities of Judea and Israel in the very nature and character of Christ. The Lion of the tribe of Judah began to manifest in and through them as every demonic predator fled before them. They discovered that their prophetic roar contained within it all the same authority and power of THE Lion, Jesus, the Lion of Judah!

All believers need to rise up and take their authority in the anointing of the Lion of Judah and begin to roar; for when they do, it is a clear reminder to the enemy that there can only be one "King of the Jungle" in heaven, in earth and under the earth! When we allow our inner lion to rise up in faith and power and roar under the anointing of "The Lion", it scatters the devil (and all his demons) and reminds them of their defeated state and their ending fate.

The next place the cherubim is mentioned is in Genesis 3 at the garden of Eden. Two cherubim stood on either side of the garden with flaming swords, keeping sinful man from reaching the tree of life, which is in the midst of the paradise of God, the source of all anointing.

"Then the Lord God said, "Behold, the man has become like one of us, to know good and evil. And now, lest he put out his hand and take also of the tree of life, and eat, and live forever. Therefore the Lord God sent him out of the garden of Eden to till the ground from which he was taken. So He drove out the man; and He placed cherubim at the east of the Garden of Eden, and a flaming sword which turned every way, to guard the way to the tree of life." (Gen. 3:22-24)

From Genesis to Revelation, the cherubim are creatures with four faces. *Four* speaks of the four corners of the earth, nations, or the globe. It also speaks of that which is plumb and of that which is full and complete. Throughout each lesson in this book, you will see and hear truths concerning the anointing that will stir the pure in heart and release the captive soul. Why the anointing? By it, the rod of punishment is removed from the shoulder of the oppressed and chains are broken. The list of accomplishments credited to the anointing continues to grow. As we search the scriptures, we find this list is inexhaustible. Isaiah 10:27 says it plainly, "It shall come to pass in that day that his burden will be taken away from your shoulder, and his yoke from your neck, and the yoke will be destroyed because of the anointing oil."

When you stop to think how many yokes, (also translated as "snares"), are prepared by our adversaries and are hurled in our direction daily, you can then grasp how many troubled hearts are made to rejoice in the promise that no weapon formed against them shall prosper. For by the anointing, every burden is destroyed. Our Savior, our Lord and Redeemer, the Chosen One, the Ancient of Days, is called the Christ, the Anointed One. Why is He called the Christ? Because He chose to do nothing of Himself but declared, "The works that I do are of the Father."

"Philip said to Him, 'Lord, show us the Father, and it is sufficient for us.' Jesus said to him, 'Have I been with you so long, and yet you have not known Me, Philip? He who has seen Me has seen the Father; so how can you say, 'Show us the Father'? Do you not believe that I am in the Father, and the Father in Me? The words that I speak to you I do not speak on My own authority; but the Father who dwells in Me does the works. Believe Me that I am in the Father and the Father in Me, or else believe Me for the sake of the works themselves.'" (John 14:8-9)

All that the Father has in possession, the riches in glory, in Christ Jesus, are now made available to all believers through faith. Where there is faith, the anointing flows. Where the Spirit of the Lord is flowing, there is liberty!

Isaiah 61:1-3 NKJV: "The Spirit of the Lord God is upon Me, Because the Lord has anointed Me to preach good tidings to the poor; He has sent Me to heal the brokenhearted, to proclaim liberty to the captives, and the opening of the prison to those who are bound; To proclaim the acceptable year of the Lord, and the day of vengeance of our God; To comfort all who mourn, to console those who mourn in Zion, to give them beauty for ashes, the oil of joy for mourning, the garment of praise for the spirit of heaviness; that they may be called trees of righteousness, the planting of the Lord after whom they may devour, that He may be glorified."

"Be sober, be vigilant; because your adversary the devil, as a roaring lion walketh about, seeking whom he may devour."
(1 Peter 5:8)

One more important factor that we must never lose sight of is that the body of Christ -- The Lion's pride, the church-- has an arch enemy, and the enemy looks just like one of the pride. For the word of God declares that the devil goes about as "a roaring lion seeking whom he may devour." No wonder believers need such ferocity in their anointing. The Lion's anointing teaches us all things and gives us a sense of great discernment. The Lion's anointing is truly an excellent anointing.

Chapter 2
The Excellent Anointing

The anointing is the most sought after blessing in Christianity, because it is a revealer of truth and the source of power. "...and where the Spirit of the Lord is, there is liberty" (2 Cor. 3:17). More plainly, there is the destroying of the yoke and the burden so the believer can walk in victory.

God's anointing has one source, but many channels. In speaking of the Holy Spirit, Jesus said, "He that believeth on Me, as the Scripture hath said, out of his belly shall flow rivers of living water" (John 7:38 KJV). One Spirit - many rivers. One person may be anointed to sing, another to preach, another to pray, and another to excel in business. The Bible depicts God anointing people to build, to make pots and vessels, fight battles, write books, and direct the army of God to do great physical exploits. It is this anointing that heals the sick, opens blind eyes, and casts out demons! All this anointing comes from one source (the Spirit of God), but the anointing seems to flow as separate rivers in each person's life. We must constantly remind ourselves that God is far too big to be confined in one manifestation of His greatness. He is God and His exceeding greatness are beyond our limited understanding. The same is true concerning His anointing.

Perhaps it would help to think of the anointing as electricity that runs through a house. It is utilized in different voltages, but it comes from the same power source. Our homes are wired for 220 volts of electricity, that we break down to 110 volts for most applications. Electricity can cool or heat the air in our homes; it can power vacuums, fans, and multiple appliances. It gives us light, music, and television. All of these things can be activated at the same time. The type of energy is always the same, but the appliance that is plugged into it determines its manifestation. Similarly, the anointing is a divine energy that may manifest in diverse ways. For instance, those anointed by the Spirit in the same service may give inspired words, render divine healing, give comfort, play exciting music, and much more. Each believer experiencing the anointing responds according to the gift that is in his or her spirit. They only need to release the power of the spirit. Just as electricity only needs for the appliance to be plugged in and turned on.

The Anointing is More Desirable than Necessary Food

The need for the anointing is obvious; we see this from Genesis to Revelation. In Genesis, The Book of Beginnings, Jacob anointed a pile of stones, marking the place where heaven touched earth. He proclaimed this place to be Bethel, the house of the Lord, the place of God's manifested presence and glory. At the end of the Bible, in the book of Revelation, we are directed to anoint our eyes with salve, so that we may see as God sees. Throughout the scriptures, God provided the anointing for the instruments He chose for His service. The O.T. tabernacle and every instrument of service in it were anointed. Aaron and his sons were anointed. Israel's prophets and kings were anointed. Even her land is called "The Holy Land," meaning it was anointed and set apart for God's sacred purposes.

God identifies with His anointed ones and they experience unusual power. Samson experienced increased physical strength.

THE EXCELLENT ANOINTING

Elijah worked various miracles because of the anointing, and his successor, Elisha pleaded with Elijah for a double portion of his anointing. As a result, he performed twice the number of miracles Elijah did. Moses' anointing was so great that he conquered Egypt with ten plagues (the number of dominion) and delivered Israel, illustrating that the anointing gives you dominion over all things. Moses, by the same anointing, received the revelation of tabernacle worship and wrote the Torah, the first five books of the Bible. David's anointing brought down Goliath and strengthened the armies of Israel to the point that they defeated every army along their borders and brought an end to war in their time. Solomon's anointing was so ear-marked by wisdom and justice that Israel enjoyed *forty years* of peace and prosperity. The greatest anointing of all was the anointing of Christ. It gave Him vicarious atoning power, so that He was able to take all the sins of the human race in His own body and nail them to the cross. At the same time, He took all of our sicknesses and sorrows and conquered them. If that wasn't enough, He took the bill of debt that was against mankind and posted it in the public square after He wrote, "cancelled" on it.

"But God demonstrates His own love toward us, in that while we were still sinners, Christ died for us." (Rom. 5:8)

"For He made Him who knew no sin to be sin for us, that we might become the righteousness of God in Him." (2 Cor. 5:21)

"And He Himself is the propitiation for our sins, and not for ours only but also for the whole world." (1 John 2:2)

This anointing on Jesus reached even further; He took the demonic, put it under His feet, and spoiled principalities and powers. The anointing upon Him was so great that He defeated

17

death, hell and the grave. Christ, the Anointed One, defeated everything that was against us at the cross. Then, in His resurrection, He rose to continually share with us the abundant, anointed and victorious life, and the all-powerful life of those set apart and sealed with the deposit of the Holy Spirit. This is the true lion's anointing, of which every believer shares in this great inheritance. We share in the riches of glory that we might walk with Him in heavenly places and that He might walk with us as the hope of glory, as the Lion of Judah; as the Lion of Light; as a lion who roars from his den; as a lion of perpetual rejoicing; as the lion that is like the Son of God who's decrees stand forever and ever, from everlasting to everlasting. The Lion's anointing is irrevocable, as the testimony of Jesus Christ is the ensign to the nations pointing to the open door of eternal glory. Amen.

What is so wonderful about the anointing that a person would find it more desirable than their necessary daily food? Over the centuries, men and women have fasted and prayed for weeks, seeking a deeper experience in the anointing. Others have denied themselves a variety of the pleasures of this world in order to enjoy the pleasures of the heavenly kingdom, which are found only in the wonderful anointing that comes through a deep relationship with Jesus Christ. Is it correct to say, "I am being anointed with the Anointing", or does the word *anointing* describe a substance, which in the natural, in most cases, is oil? Either way, the anointing is the Holy Spirit, and the only One who is doing the anointing. The Holy Spirit chose to anoint whoever or whatever was in need of His anointing, whether that was by the oil poured out from the horn of Samuel the prophet over young David's head to be anointed the new King of Israel over his brothers, or when Sampson and his donkey jaw bone was anointed to engage in battle with the Philistine armies, or when Mary Magdalene broke her precious alabaster jar filled

18

with expensive oils and poured it over Jesus' head and anointed Him with this sacrifice and her tears and then dried His feet with her hair. God knows what a person means when they use the word "anointing" even if they use it in the wrong tense.

"Now he who keeps His commandments abides in Him, and He in him. And by this we know that He abides in us, by the Spirit whom He has given us." (1 John 3:24)

The Anointing Breaks Every Yoke

The first yoke the anointing destroys is the super-perfectionism that comes out of the "holier than thou" attitude of church organizations, which manifests itself in self-criticism, and criticism of others. This attitude causes some people to believe that when they are anointed, they will be perfect. The only perfect anointed One is Jesus, for the Father hath made Him both Lord, and Christ (Acts 2:36 KJV)

The O.T. shows that the sweet oil that was used to anoint those who ministered in the service of the altar was a blend of olive oil and six spices. This oil, in its narrowest application, is symbolic of the Holy Spirit. The Holy Spirit is equally symbolized in a much broader application of types, in the scripture by rain, dew, rivers of water, and streams in the desert. Other symbols used to characterize the Holy Spirit in the scriptures are new wine, wind, fire, smoke, and the cloud of God's presence (cloud of Glory) in the tabernacle. The word *anointing* is generally used in the scriptures as a verb. It is also occasionally used as a noun. In its verb form, it is *anoint*, which speaks of applying oil to the vessel being set apart and empowered for God's service. The noun form speaks of the Holy Spirit, both the reality of His presence, and the fact that He is at work, manifesting the supernatural things of Jesus Christ through the gifts and the fruit of His Spirit. The

ANOINTED TO ROAR

Holy Spirit is omnipresent, yet we do not always sense His presence. When the word   is used as a noun, it describes the manifested presence of the Holy Spirit in a form we can respond to through faith.

Sometimes both the verb and the noun are used. The noun tells us the Holy Spirit is present. The verb tells us the presence of the Holy Spirit is working effectively, "...that we might have life, and that more abundantly" (John 10:10). Since the verb form means "to apply" or minister the Holy Spirit to someone, you could properly say, "Brother Needy is being anointed by prayer and prophecy, or prayer and exhortation, or prayer and praises." You could say, "I saw the anointing come on him and break the yoke and destroy the burden and heal the broken hearted." The verb form, which is the act of administering the oil (the Holy Spirit) to someone, includes everything from a drop of oil to pouring a pitcher of oil on the one being anointed. In the priestly anointing of Moses' day, a drop of oil was applied to the toe, the thumb of the right hand, and the ear. The big toe is the guiding toe on the foot we put forward. In anointing the priest's big toe with oil, the priest's walk would be anointed. Just as the thumb is the instrument of strength on the right hand, the anointing of the priest's thumb empowered him for strength in his service. Similarly, a drop of oil on the priest's ear anointed him to hear what the Spirit was saying. The same provision is still available for New Testament (N.T.) believers. The Spirit wants to anoint and energize our walk, our service, and our hearing. Without this anointing, it is impossible for us to walk in faith, serve acceptably, or speak as God's mouthpiece. The word *anointing* also implies "brushing." If the priest, upon whom the oil was poured, should happen to walk by the needy and his garments even brushed them ever so slightly, they would be blessed. In the book of Acts, we see the same principle as the Apostle Peter was walking through the streets of Jerusalem where the sick people were laying. Peter was so anointed that everyone was healed even as his shadow passed and brushed over some.

"And through the hands of the apostles many signs and wonders were done among the people. And they were all with one accord in Solomon's Porch. Yet none of the rest dared join them, but the people esteemed them highly. And believers were increasingly added to the Lord, multitudes of both men and women, so that they brought the sick out into the streets and laid them on beds and couches, that at least the shadow of Peter passing by might fall on some of them." (Acts 5:12-15)

On one occasion, I remember when my mentor, Pastor Glen Foster, came out of the prayer room to the pulpit to preach. He was so saturated with the anointing that the person sitting closest to where he was walking fell out of his chair in the Spirit. The pianist fell off the piano bench as he brushed by, and the people on the front row of the church fell onto the floor in the Spirit. I have seen prayer lines where the anointed minister just walked by without touching anyone, yet it was like the minister had a flowing garment that just brushed the people and they all fell under the power of the anointing. I have personally ministered in crusades, in Asian countries like Myanmar Burma, Manila Philippines, and Singapore where I was so saturated with the anointing. As I began to pray for the crowds of people coming to the altar, I would begin to lift my right hand up to lay my hands on the tops of their heads to pray for their needs. The very tips of my fingers would barely brush against their foreheads and they would gasp and fall out in the power of the Spirit of God onto the hard concrete floor beneath them; yet when they landed it was as if they fell onto a bed of down feathers.

The anointing can also be transferred by hearing a person's name, as David said, "You have delivered me from the strivings of the people; you have made me the head of the nations; A people I have not known shall serve me. As soon as they hear of me they obey me; the foreigners submit to me" (Ps. 18:44). Those who minister in the prophetic gifts have found that as their eyes make contact with a person who is being ministered to and being sought out by the Spirit of God, there is an impartation of knowledge, wisdom, and power given to them for that particular person.

The act of anointing also includes smearing the oil. For example, the Apostle James talks about anointing the sick with oil. "Is anyone among you sick? Let him call for the elders of the church, and let them pray over him, anointing him with oil in the name of the Lord" (Jas. 5:14). This particular phrase,"Anointing him with oil," means a "smearing and rubbing in." Quite often, a minister, when praying for and ministering healing to the sick, will smear holy oil on the forehead of the one he is ministering to. Once in a while, the minister may be led to smear the oil on the exact spot of the ailment, such as a broken ankle. Of course, rubbing a particular oil on it does not heal a broken ankle, but the oil represents the power of the Holy Spirit, and the rubbing in represents the penetration of the supernatural anointing that works miracles! The verb form of the anointing also includes pouring the oil on the head, so that it runs down all over the garments. David poetically illustrates this when he wrote: "Behold, how good and how pleasant it is for brethren to dwell together in unity! It is like the precious oil upon the head, running down on the beard, the beard of Aaron, Running down on the edge of his garments" (Ps. 133:1-2).

THE EXCELLENT ANOINTING

Whether a drop of oil or a pitcher full, in the verb form or the noun form, the anointing is precious, priceless, perfect, and peace giving. It is through the anointing that faith rises and promises become a reality. What's so wonderful about the anointing? It is a discernible form of the invisible God in whose presence is the fullness of joy. It is a supernatural power touching natural people, transforming us into new creatures and giving us supernatural access to all the riches in glory, in Christ Jesus. This anointing, the oil of heaven, is so often ministered to us through the Word of God. As we hear it, think on it, wait for it; like natural oil soaks into the hair, the skin, the garments, this heavenly oil soaks into the mind, heart, soul, emotions, and even the physical body. It brings transformation to people's lives and allows the supernatural to be absorbed by the natural so that death is swallowed up in victory. The Word reveals the anointing and the anointing reveals the truth of the Word. So wonderful is this process that there is a washing and liberating effect similar to reverse osmosis. Truly the anointing breaks the yoke and destroys every burden. Whether we are seeking information for the mind, understanding for the heart, revelation for the spirit, or manifestation for the physical, the wonderful anointing makes the difference.

No wonder Jesus said, "But tarry ye in the city of Jerusalem [peace] until you are endued with power from on high" (Luke 24:49 KJV). Under the law we are sanctified by the blood, the water (the Word), and the fine anointing oils. The anointing oil – the Holy Spirit – by which spiritual things are made comprehensible to the simplest believer, touches almost everything in our Christian life. Though the natural man does not understand the things of the Spirit of God (they are foolishness to him), God reveals them to us in His anointing. The most wonderful thing of all about the anointing, is that God has made it available to all believers, which He pours upon and within. No one has more available to them than anyone else. We all have access daily to a generational anointing that touches every area of our lives and we all have access to special anointing for special situations when needed. Thank God for the wonderful anointing!

Chapter 3
All Believers Are Anointed

The anointing does not belong only to the professionals of religion. No ordination certificate is necessary. All believers are anointed- making them usable instruments in the hands of God. All who put their faith in Jesus Christ are anointed by God and established with Christ and the apostles in God's eternal purposes.

"Now He who establishes us with you in Christ and has anointed us is God, who also has sealed us and given us the Spirit in our hearts as a guarantee." (2 Cor. 1:21-22 NKJV)

N.T. believers are promised a total baptism – a complete immersion in the Holy Spirit – God's anointing oil. The oil of the Spirit imparts super-human power, to hear, think, speak, walk and minister as Jesus, our pattern Anointed One did. Because of the anointing, we can do not only the works that Jesus did, but greater works.

"Most assuredly, I say to you, he who believes in Me, the works that I do he will do also; and greater works than these he will do, because I go to My Father." (John 14:12)

God gives us an anointing to think with the mind of Christ, the Anointed One, and to minister with His power while walking in His victory. The anointing enables every believer to share in the defeat of God's enemies. When we walk in this anointing on the job, in the home, or in any facet of life, we release the sweet smelling savor of the knowledge of His victory in every place.

"Now thanks be to God who always leads us in triumph in Christ, and through us diffuses the fragrance of His knowledge in every place. For we are to God the fragrance of Christ among those who are being saved and among those who are perishing. To the one we are the aroma of death leading to death, and to the other the aroma of life leading to life." (2 Cor. 2:14-16)

"Pleasing is the fragrance of your perfumes; your name is like perfume poured out. No wonder the young women love you!" (Song of Songs 1:3)

The anointing is the source of wisdom, mercy, prophecy, grace, discerning of spirits, and long suffering. Joy, peace, a word of knowledge, the gifts of healing, and the diverse kinds of tongues are also accompanying works of the anointing. Faith, miracles, self-discipline, gentleness, brotherly kindness, interpretation of tongues, goodness, faithfulness, and love are direct results of the Holy Spirit's presence in the life of a believer. It is one anointing but with different manifestations. This anointing that we have received is not here today and gone tomorrow; it is an abiding anointing, reflecting permanence of the Spirit's indwelling ministry in our lives. The anointing is always resident in us, teaching us to abide in Christ the Anointed One. The apostle John affirmed: "But the anointing which you have received of Him abideth in you..." (1 John 2:27 KJV).

With a prophetic eye that saw a day of greater anointing than O.T. believers had ever experienced, Isaiah prophetically roared out some 700 hundred years into the future and said, "The spirit of the Lord GOD is upon me; because the LORD hath anointed me to preach good tidings unto the meek; he hath sent me to bind up the brokenhearted, to proclaim liberty to the captives, and the opening of the prison to them that are bound" (Isa. 61:1 KJV).

It was the anointing upon Isaiah's life that enabled and empowered him to prophetically roar into the future destiny of the earth; the promise of the coming of the long awaited Messiah – Jesus. The anointing that roared out from this man kept this prophetic promise alive and surging with power for approximately 700 years until the very moment that the earth's prophetic destiny aligned with God's appointed time and season. This portion of Scripture was fulfilled when Jesus read aloud in the synagogue of His own hometown of Nazareth; "The Spirit of the Lord is upon Me, Because He has anointed Me to preach the gospel to the poor; He has sent Me to heal the brokenhearted, to proclaim liberty to the captives and recovery of sight to the blind, to set at liberty those who are oppressed; to proclaim the acceptable year of the Lord" (Luke 4:18-19). But the Lion of Judah didn't stop roaring there; he then added this phrase that not only sealed Isaiah's prophecy, but would forever radically change the course of the world's history, "…today this Scripture is fulfilled in your hearing." (Luke 4:21)

At the beginning of Jesus' ministry, when the heaven opened and the visible dove of the Spirit descended upon Christ at His water baptism, He obtained access to the anointing for ministry, for all believers, for all time. The Church never needs to walk without power, for Jesus said: "Fear not, little flock, for it is your Father's good pleasure to give you the kingdom" (Luke 12:32 KJV). It is consistent with the teaching of Jesus that the Father is more willing to give us the anointing than we are anxious to receive it. Jesus (Christ) is the Anointed One. He is the cornerstone of the anointed life. Even in the sign and wonder generation of Moses' ministry, nothing could even compare with the anointing that rested upon Christ Jesus. When the Holy Spirit is upon us in any measure, the power is present to preach or proclaim the message that it is His provision that brings our help and our complete deliverance. However, preaching is only one work of the anointing.

In his prophecy, Isaiah spoke of seven works of the anointing:
1. To heal the brokenhearted
2. To proclaim liberty to the captives
3. To open the prison doors to those who are bound
4. To proclaim the acceptable year of the Lord
5. To proclaim the day of vengeance of our God
6. To comfort all who mourn (especially those who mourn in Zion)
7. To grant an assignment of "recovery" on four levels
   a) beauty for ashes
   b) the oil of joy for mourning
   c) the garment of praise for the spirit of heaviness
   d) to be planted as trees of righteousness, to glorify His name (see Isa. 61:1-3)

The Anointing Is Found In The Anointer

The anointing oil symbolically represents the Holy Spirit. We may lose sight of this truth if our focus is on the outworking, or manifestation of the anointing. We cannot separate the anointing from the anointer, the Spirit of God, who is its source. The divine Holy Spirit, the third person of the Godhead, is the possessor of the divine nature in equality with the Father and the Son. He is constantly at work in our lives, producing holiness and the fruit of the Spirit. Based on my many years of being a pastor, I have discovered that many people mentally reverse the order of the

Spirit's true operation. They think we must produce holiness and then, as a special reward, God anoints us. Nothing could be further from the truth. While it is true that God is a rewarder of them that diligently seek Him (Heb. 11:6), the gift of the Holy Spirit is just that: it is a 'gift' and not a reward (or something you earn). He is our helper; He comes to us by promise. We receive Him, not by our good works, but by faith. During Peter's very first anointed sermon on the day of Pentecost, under the unction of the anointing of the Holy Spirit, like a mighty lion, Peter roared out these powerful words; "…repent, and be baptized every one of you in the name of Jesus Christ for the remission of sins, and ye shall receive the gift of the Holy Spirit. For the promise is unto you, and to your children, and to all that are afar off, even as many as the Lord our God shall call." (Acts 2:38-39)

Paul, when writing to the Galatians, made it explicitly clear that the presence, power, and anointing of the Holy Spirit is not a reward, but a free gift to all who believe. He told them, and us, "Christ hath redeemed us from the curse of the law, being made a curse for us: for it is written, Cursed is every one that hangeth on a tree: That the blessing of Abraham might come on the gentiles through Jesus Christ; that we might receive the promise of the Spirit through faith." (Gal. 3:13-14 KJV)

Jesus said that the only condition for the coming of the Holy Spirit upon all flesh was His return to the Father. His exact words were: "Nevertheless I tell you the truth; it is expedient for you that I go away: for if I go not away, the Comforter will not come unto you; but if I depart, I will send him unto you." (John 16:7)

The Anointing Is Universal
In Joel's great prophecy about the last days, God declared, "And it shall come to pass afterward, that I will pour out of my Spirit

upon all flesh; and your sons and your daughters shall prophesy, your old men shall dream dreams, your young men shall see visions." (Joel 2:28). On the day of Pentecost, following the resurrection of Jesus, when Jews from all over Asia were gathered for the great feast day, God poured His Spirit upon the patiently waiting believers in the Upper Room.

"And there were dwelling in Jerusalem Jews, devout men, from every nation under heaven. And when this sound occurred, the multitude came together, and were confused, because everyone heard them speak in his own language. Then they were all amazed and marveled, saying to one another, 'Look, are not all these who speak Galilaeans? And how is it that we hear, each in our own language in which we were born? (vs. 11) … We hear them speaking in our own tongues the wonderful works of God.'" So they were all amazed and perplexed, saying to one another, "Whatever could this mean?" (Acts 2:5-12)

In his explanatory sermon, Peter declared that "…this is that which was spoken by the prophet Joel…" (Acts 2:16), and he proceeded to quote the Joel prophecy. His application of Joel 2:28 had many implications, for it declared that the anointing (the presence and power of the Holy Spirit) that had previously been restricted to certain persons and offices in the O.T., was now available to ALL believers. To the Jews this was revolting; to others this was revolutionary. To the believers, it was revelatory! God was saying that none are excluded from a special anointing. "All flesh" could be anointed for Christian living. All persons could enjoy freedom from the bondage of sin, the burdens of life, and the blindness of the carnal nature by the power of God's multifaceted anointing. Anyone could be anointed by the Spirit for Christian work and service. Anyone could operate in the lion's anointing. We are anointed to roar in power, authority, and dominion. The Lion of the tribe of Judah made it possible for us ALL to operate in the lion's anointing.

The Anointing Is Relational

The book of Acts says that the early believers were first called "Christians" at Antioch. The word *Christ* means, "The Anointed One." The word *Christian* means, "Christ-like." A true Christian, then, is one who shares the anointing of Jesus out of relationship with Him. Knowing that those who believed on Him would be anointed with the Holy Spirit, Jesus said, "…he that believeth on Me, the works that I do shall he do also; and greater works than these shall he do; because I go unto my Father" (John 14:12 KJV). This has become more than a mere promise, for Jesus went to the Father as the great High Priest of our profession, who ever lives to make intercession for us (Heb. 7:25). His presence in heaven is our assurance that the rubbing in of the anointing oil is a continual experience. He never leaves us nor forsakes us. Jesus is always directing the Holy Spirit to be manifested throughout the body of Christ for all ages until His return. He came the first time as the Lamb of God; He comes again as the Lion of the tribe of Judah. Two thousand years ago, the religious leaders shouted in scorn, "He saved others, but he can't save himself!" (Matt. 27:42). The day is coming when the whole world will see Jesus as He really is; The Lion. When that happens, every knee will bow and every tongue confess that Jesus Christ is Lord, to the glory of God the Father. (Phil. 2:9-11)

The anointing we enjoy is not actually our anointing, but the anointing of the Son of God, whose throne is established forever. We must never take the anointing as a sign that God is exalting us, approving us, or drawing attention to us. The manifestation of the Spirit, which is the anointing at work in us and through us, is to show how highly exalted the Son of God is in our lives and all attention should only be given to Him. The more we endeavor to "...keep the unity of the Spirit in the bond of peace..." And function as "...one body, and one Spirit, even as ye are called in one hope of your calling, one Lord, one faith, one baptism, one God and Father of all, who is above all, and through all, and in you all..." For "...unto every one of us is given grace according to the measure of the gift of Christ..." (Eph. 4:3-7), the more the Spirit's anointing will be manifested among us. We all have this anointing, but when we function together, we are like the multiple facets of a diamond in radiating dazzling beauty. The diamond is not the beauty, but because of its relationship to light, it displays the radiance of the color spectrum. Similarly, we are not the beauty of God, but by our relationship to the Anointed One, Christ Jesus, our divine anointing, we can exhibit the excellencies of the nature of God. Now it is God who establishes us together in the Anointed One; sharing that anointing with us. He has sealed us and deposited an ample supply of the anointing in our hearts (2 Cor. 1:21-22). We learn to stay under its influence, to stay in its flow, and to stay in touch with its power. In other words, it's not about how loudly *we* can roar within ourselves, but it's about how loudly *The Lion* is roaring within our own hearts that impels us to roar!

The Anointing Is Disruptive

Those who learn to live in an anointing are never the same again. Their lives become favorably different, and the lives of those around them are affected. For example, look at Moses; his life was changed forever, and the lives of everyone around him were disrupted by the anointing he received at the burning bush. By the anointing, God not only ordered the release of His people, but the anointing caused the rod of Moses and Aaron to swallow up the rods of the magicians (which symbolizes demonic counterfeit of the true anointing). This special anointing brought an end to the work of the sorcerers. At the same time, the anointing was destroying the idols and magicians in Egypt. It was destroying the fear, hopelessness and sentence of death upon the head of each Israelite. While the anointing was irritating the Egyptians, it was comforting the Israelites. The more the Egyptians persecuted the Israelites, the more the Israelites prospered and grew. Yokes were broken by the anointing (Ex. 3). By the rod of power, God brought all Israel out of the land of Egypt. The greatest miracle of Israel's deliverance was the strength the anointing gave to the people to believe in their deliverance. It gave them courage to put the lamb's blood on their doorposts, and rely solely upon God to bring them out of Egypt the following morning. Thus, by the anointing, the people escaped from the destruction of Egypt.

The lesson to be learned today is that the anointing destroys personal bondages, national bondages, and international bondages. This is why Jesus said to His disciples: "Go therefore and make disciples of all the nations, baptizing them in the name of the Father and of the Son and of the Holy Spirit, teaching them to observe all things that I have commanded you; and lo, I am with you always, even to the end of the age" (Matt. 28:19-20). Jesus knew that the power to destroy all bondage would be in the sending and in the anointing of the Holy Spirit and that the promise of this bondage breaking anointing would be released in power on the Day of Pentecost. "But you shall receive power when the Holy Spirit has come upon you; and you shall be witnesses to Me in Jerusalem, and in all Judea and Samaria, and to the end of the earth." (Acts 1:8)

Anointed people make the difference on all levels of human existence. Where the anointing goes, the glory goes. When the anointing is recognized, miracles are made possible. When the anointing is released, prisoners are set free. Those who keep in memory that there is an anointing that always abides and teaches us all things will discover that it is a rod of authority that destroys the wicked one. "For this purpose the Son of God was manifested, that He might destroy the works of the devil." (1 John 3:8)

The church must grasp the understanding that the anointing is far more than a message of holiness within the house of God. It is a rod of power to destroy wicked governments, industries, false teachers, false churches, and deceptive customs that would hold men under tyrannical rule of any type. The anointing has come to set the captives free!

The Anointing Is Individualistic

The same anointing on two persons will usually produce two separate courses of action. It is like one source of electricity empowering whatever appliance is plugged into it. The Holy Spirit uses our different personalities, backgrounds, training and abilities. The anointing was a rod of power to Moses, a mantle to Elijah, a song of triumph to Deborah, and supernatural strength to Samson. From Samson to Esther, those who learned to receive the Lion's anointing- and released it- have contributed to the deliverance of their generation and the building up of the kingdom of God. Some were well-known; others came out of obscurity, but all knew God in a close, personal fellowship, which is the ultimate effect of the anointing.

Chapter 4
The Ever-Increasing Glory

All believers have within their reach the opportunity to increase the effective work of the anointing in their lives. The book of Zechariah, declares that victory does not come through military power or war in the flesh. "...not by might, nor by power, but by My Spirit, says the LORD of hosts" (Zech. 4:6). The defeat of worldwide communism was accomplished in the streets of Moscow without so much as a gun being fired. This generation was chosen to be an eyewitness to what no other generation has ever been permitted to see - the move of the Holy Spirit over the military governments of this world. The first recorded incident in Bible history where the minds of men were influenced and changed by the tri-unity of heaven, rather than by bullets and guns, took place at the account of the Tower of Babel (Gen. 11). The story is very simple; the scripture says that the Lord came down to see the city and the great tower that men had built up to the heavens (some scholars identify the tower in this narrative as the three-hundred-foot high temple Ziggurat of Marduk at Babylon). This description suggests a monumental effort made by human beings, motivated by pride in a titanic attempt at corporate self-assertion, sacrilegiously challenging God to make a name for themselves. Since a name connotes fame and progeny, these city builders were attempting to find significance and immortality in their own ingenious, unified achievements. Only God gives an everlasting name to those who magnify His name. Like Cain, in their isolation from God, these proud sinners feared dislocation or becoming vagabonds. Also like Cain, they found their solution in an abiding city rivaling God—a strategy that involved disobeying God's command to "fill the earth" (Gen. 9:1). But God saw this attempt to create a massive stairway to the heavens and breathed on mortal flesh, confusing their languages and, "The Lord scattered them abroad from thence over the face of all the earth, and they ceased building the city" (Gen. 11:8). There is no record of what they said on that day, but we do know they did not kill each other. We know that people were scattered and gathered in their own chosen lands, just as churches with similar doctrines or cultures gather together in different places today.

Later on in history, God permitted His people to be carried away into captivity on several occasions. For instance, when Jacob (the father of Joseph) went to live in Egypt, he and his people were given the best farmlands and cities in the land of Goshen, without their armies having to fight a war. The Holy Spirit simply moved upon the government, and in the process brought Joseph from the king's dungeon to sit with the king on the throne. From the very beginning, Joseph declared to the Pharaoh that he in himself had no skills to interpret his dream. He was quick to inform Pharaoh that man cannot do what he asked, but there is a God in heaven who knows ALL things, and who can do ALL things. He showed Joseph what the king's dream represented. The anointing in Joseph's life overcame all obstacles. It not only ministered through Joseph, it also ministered through Pharaoh. "Ministered through Pharaoh? How could that be?" Egypt, at that time, had the largest military government on earth. It was the greatness of this government that brought the story of Joseph's anointing, and how it saved several nations from famine, and brought the nation of Israel to the attention of the entire world. As we now know, it was for that very purpose that God sent Israel into Egypt. It was the anointing that flowed from father Abraham that effectively altered all the families on the earth. The nations of the earth, in general, were ruled by tyrannical leaders who used and abused the people of their societies. When Joseph came to power at Pharaoh's side, he began to teach the people the ways of God. He began to teach them about the existence of the living God. He revealed to them a different kind of government. He showed them that they, with God's help, could bless one another. This teaching totally changed the outlook of many nations. These nations learned from the earliest beginnings of antiquity that it is better to give than to receive; the more anointing, the more blessing.

All the good things we read about in Genesis came out of the anointing. When the time came for Israel to go into the Promised Land, the Lord gave the word that it was time for them to come out of the house of bondage. Immediately the king said, "Who is the Lord that I should obey him?" It was about to be illustrated to the nations of the earth the truth that the anointing cannot be franchised, bought or sold, nor can it be owned or controlled by any one man; it is a free gift. When the anointing is used for the furtherance of God's purposes among the nations, there are miracles, signs and wonders that follow. In fact, with Moses there were ten major plagues and innumerable acts of mercy and power as God brought him and the children of Israel out of Egypt and across the Red Sea. At the Red Sea, is where Egypt learned that the anointing, which is invisible, is more powerful than any army on the earth. God took everything in the wilderness, which was ugly and hard to deal with, and turned it into a blessing! The dream of freedom, one nation under God, endowed with faith and hope for a generation to come. It was Israel who would learn the ways of God in a wilderness, and become the Lion's roar as one generation after another rose to power. Each generation watched the potential glory slip through their fingers as they stumbled over lost identities. To be sure that the anointing would be appreciated and highly valued, God made known His plan, little by little, which had been kept secret from the beginning of the world. (See Eph. 3:5)

The anointing flows into each human life one drop at a time. The picture in Zechariah 4 of two olive trees, teaches us how the anointing flows like oil; out of the olive tree and into pipes, then into the believer who is the lamp of the Spirit. The scope of this anointing reaches unto the ends of the earth, as Isaiah 11:9 said, "… For the earth shall be full of the knowledge of the Lord, as the waters cover the sea." The knowledge of the scriptures comes by study and by revelation. All scripture is inspirational and when we are exposed to its infinite light, the anointing from its glowing glory breaks the yoke and destroys every burden. Meditating on the Word of God will increase the outflow of the light of glory in every believer.

Psalms 133 declares, that where there is unity among worshippers, the anointing glory comes down like the dew on Mt. Hermon. Now, Mt. Hermon (Mt. Zion - Deut. 4:48), is among the Mount Calvary chain of high places surrounding Jerusalem. Thus, when the glory of the anointing is manifested, Calvary the place of the cross is visible. Mt. Hermon (the place of devotion) and Mount Olivet (the place of abundant illumination) are illuminated, and then we, like mirrors, reflect the glory into the city of Jerusalem.

Psalms 133 talks about the dew that drops down onto Mt. Hermon. We find from the study of the Hebrew that the dew is a prophetic revelation. The text actually says, "The prophetic revelation distills like dew." This is what takes place in the anointing of the High Priest. There were so many drops of oil falling on Aaron that it became like oil poured out of a vessel onto Aaron's head, down over his hair, through his beard, onto his vestures, and down to the tips of his garments. This is like being baptized in oil, which is symbolic of the baptism of the Holy Spirit. A person who has been touched with this kind of anointing is saturated with an understanding and wisdom that is far above and beyond the ordinary perception. You cannot have this saturation anointing without an abundance of illumination. This is only attainable through meditating on the Word of God day and night. In order to get the anointing out of some olive branches, you have to wait for years for the growth of wisdom and knowledge. Thus, the anointing breaks the yoke and destroys the burden, making it possible for us to be built up on the most holy faith (Jesus). Praying in the Holy Spirit, being led of the Spirit from glory to glory, comes about through an understanding which the apostle John declares, "But you have an unction from the Holy One, and you know all things." (1 John 2:20)

As we venture outward from our earthly religious life, we pass into the heavenlies, and like Ezekiel of old, we can have eyes to see into the invisible realm. Most people just live on the fringes of the anointing. Every revival recorded in history is God's attempt to bring us out of our earth-bound lifestyle and into the supernatural realm of the Spirit. As we lift up our eyes, and as we begin to move our spiritual wings of praise, we are lifted up. As we begin to be lifted up from the earthly realm, we can then see things in our lives from a different perspective. We can now see the profoundness of the glory that is coming from the throne of God. We are now venturing into the realm of pure wisdom and knowledge where each step forward is also a step upward, and all knowledge from the previous levels gives way, and we, beholding the glory of God in the face of Jesus Christ, are lifted up into a heavenly realm, so that we may boldly say, "All things are under our feet." All things in the earthly realm are done according to the pattern of the heavenly realm. At this point, we can say that we have made the complete circle of the anointing graces. Furthermore, we can say that we go into the battle of the earthly realm (where spirit fights flesh) the spirit takes dominion and enters into the realm fully equipped with all aspects of the anointing. The light of the knowledge of the glory of God in the face of Jesus Christ is freely given to all believers. The Father holds nothing back. The only things that are held back from us are held back by our own fleshly nature.

Each drop of oil that falls on Mt. Hermon increases the vision capacity of the prophetic ministry of Jesus Christ, and those who have His testimony, "...for the testimony of Jesus is the spirit of prophecy" (Rev. 9:10). As discussed in a previous chapter, in the book of Revelation and Ezekiel, we are told about the cherubim. Let's take a quick look at Ezekiel 10 to examine some prophetic revelation. "Now the cherubim were standing on the south side of the temple when the man went in, and the cloud filled the inner court. Then the glory of the Lord went up from the cherub, and paused over the threshold of the temple; and the house was filled with the cloud, and the court was full of the brightness of the Lord's glory. And the sound of the wings of the cherubim was heard even in the outer court, like the voice of Almighty God when He speaks." (Ez. 10:3-5)

Concerning prophetic revelation as an interpretation, spiritual things speak of things in the natural, and natural things speak of things in the spirit. Prophetically speaking, the cherubim minister in the heavenly and the earthly sanctuaries. The earthly is always the exact replica of the heavenly. The cherubim in the earthly realm are you and I, people who love God so much that they praise Him day and night. These ones who praise are birthed out of the coals of fire and drops of oil, (the two forms of prophetic revelation). They become such lovers of God by absorbing these drops of oil and coals of fire, which causes those who are partakers of the divine nature to be changed from glory to glory into the image of Jesus Christ. As we learn to praise the Lord day and night, we will move into deeper depths and higher heights, and we will escape the corruption that is in the world through the lusts of the flesh. After Ezekiel saw the great revelation of the throne, he was shown the sign on the foreheads of those who were chosen to escape the coming destruction.

"Now the glory of the God of Israel had gone up from the cherub, where it had been, to the threshold of the temple. And He called to the man clothed with linen, who had the writer's inkhorn at his side; and the Lord said to him, 'Go through the midst of the city, through the midst of Jerusalem, and put a mark on the foreheads of the men who sigh and cry over all the abominations that are done within it.' To the others He said in my hearing, 'Go after him through the city and kill; do not let your eye spare, nor have any pity. Utterly slay old and young men, maidens and little children and women; but do not come near anyone on whom is the mark; and begin at My sanctuary.'" (Ez. 9:3-6)

In Ezekiel, chapter 10, the angel said to the messenger of Yahweh, "Go and put your hand in between the cherubim on the brazen altar and take out some coals of fire, and scatter them over the city of Jerusalem" (Rev. 10:3-5). But in Ezekiel 9, we are shown for the first time the power of the cross in connection with the cherubim. The word of the book of Ezekiel is a word that describes a transition from praisers to worshippers; from those who are drawn to God to those who are sent by God. All followers of Jesus Christ are ever being drawn into God's ongoing plans for His kingdom to come, His will to be done, on earth as in heaven. We are now the anointed ones - that army of believers who follow the Captain of the Army of Hosts wherever He goes and marches into battle. Jesus is the Lion of the tribe of Judah, and He will bring His armies to fight all those who are against the purpose of God.

In the story of Jacob, we are told that he saw a ladder which reached heaven. Using the Jacob interpretation of a ladder, Ezekiel saw his ladder was so high that it reached the throne of God. From the story of Jacob we learn that there is a permanent connection between Bethel (the house of God on earth), and the throne of God in heaven. The angels were descending (which indicates that God was initiating this fellowship), and ascending (which indicates that there is a permanent pathway between heaven and earth, so that the heavenly kingdom might come, and that we might learn to apply heavenly principles to earthly problems). The lesson to be learned from the transfiguration of Christ, the cloud coming down on the mountain, the voice that spoke out of heaven and sent them to minister the power of the heavenly in the earth; is that earth's problems are better solved by the pattern seen in the heavenly instruments. It is by the anointing from the heavenlies that God breaks the yoke in the earthly. The anointing, said Isaiah, breaks the yoke and destroys the burden, and thereby, we live in a realm beyond the struggle of the flesh. For this reason, we are instructed to seek for an ever increasing anointing, and to surrender ourselves to God through the Spirit in all things.

THE EVER INCREASING GLORY

Receiving and Releasing the Anointing

We receive the anointing the same way we receive salvation – as a free gift; "...the anointing you received from him remains in you..." (1 John 2:27). Not only are human beings created to be the dwelling place of Jesus Christ, we are also fashioned by the hand of God to be a vessel filled with the Holy Oil. When it comes to salvation, most of us have been taught to receive the person of Christ into that prepared place in the Spirit (and to receive Him as an act of faith) that we have little or no difficulty opening the door of the heart, inviting in the Christ, and envisioning His triumphal takeover of our redeemed soul. Why then should we find it difficult to receive the knowledge of the presence of the Spirit? The obstruction we encounter is the understanding that receiving is a work of faith. Most people I have conversed with on this subject look for a goose bump sensation, a warm glow, a jolt like an electrical charge, or perhaps a surge of the Spirit that knocks one to the floor; others may seek a great quiet and calm. However, all of these things are in the realm of feeling and sensation. Actually, the anointing is received, maintained, and released (at times) with no feeling at all. The effect of the presence of the Holy Spirit is seen in the fruit and the gifts of the Spirit, and the working of all righteousness.

When we believe, we receive. This applies not only to our salvation; it also applies to all that God has provided. He has made His provisions and blessings available, and we receive them when we believe. God is working in our midst by innumerable means, teaching us to receive and release His Spirit in greater and more productive ways. Faith comes by hearing the Word, not by fleshly sensations- although physical responses are neither wrong nor uncommon. The Word teaches us that just as we died to sin with Christ, as by His stripes we were healed, we have also been anointed with Him. Therefore, if we have been anointed, then *we are anointed*. If we are anointed, that anointing will teach us all things. It is a matter of learning, not earning. The more we learn of His grace, the more faith we have to see His face. The more we yield to His call, the less we struggle and the more we bubble. Too many people think of the anointing as an exterior power only. The greater truth is that the Spirit abides within all believers, waiting to be released.

Jesus said, that the world cannot receive the Holy Spirit because they cannot see Him. But to believers, He said they would see Him because He was with them (exterior) and would be in them (interior). As your belief in the existence of the Holy Spirit grows and becomes unshakable, you will see signs of godliness, self-control and peace; both on the outside and the inside. Some Christians speak as if the Holy Spirit is somewhere else rather than dwelling within them. Christ's teaching in John chapter 13-17 explicitly declares: "The Holy Spirit is here. He is present. He is not only with us, He is in us. He is not in us for only a little while. Jesus says He abides with us forever. From the day of our salvation, when the Holy Spirit moved into our temple, He began to take more and more control." If we believe this, simply because the Bible says so, it will be much easier to receive the knowledge of His presence and to yield to His desire to release works of grace and power through us. Jesus stood in the midst of the disciples, breathed on them, and said, "Receive the Holy Spirit" (John 20:22). Breathing on the disciples was a symbolic gesture on Christ's part, illustrating that the same way the lungs receive and release air, so the human spirit receives and releases the Holy Spirit. The simple acknowledgment that the Spirit is here because the Word says so puts us in a position to receive from God. It could be that He touches our mortal bodies and we feel good all over. Perhaps we experience some sort of tingling sensation that acts as a signal to get our attention. These attention-getters are signals from the spirit-man to the conscious mind, saying, "Be alert and respond to the moving of the Spirit!"

In Galatians 6:1, the Apostle Paul speaks of "...you who are spiritual." The word *spiritual* here literally means "alert and responding to the Holy Spirit." The anointing can actually be felt – although absence of feeling does not mean absence of the anointing or the Holy Spirit. God has used many methods over the years to get my attention and inform me of His desire to release some spiritual gift or some other work of His Spirit through me to a needy person. I realize that others may not respond to or experience the anointing in the same way that I do; our experiences can vary. But I believe that perhaps people could benefit from me relating some of my experiences, as well as from other people's experiences. I only give these examples to correlate each experience with various ways the word *anointing* is used in Scripture.

We could say there are three steps in this process:
1. Recognize His prompting.
2. Receive His words or instructions.
3. Release them to the person or group of people He indicates.

Several times I have felt numbness or other sensations in specific parts of my body when the Spirit was moving to release healings in the congregation. Once, early in my ministry, I felt my heart beating rapidly. I was instantly aware of an overwhelming power and realized God wanted my attention. Then a thought was revealed to my conscious mind: "I want you to speak out in tongues." When I did, an edifying interpretation followed. I have heard others speak of an upward pressure coming from the center of their being like a "bubbling up" sensation when they sense the Spirit moves them to give a word of prophecy or other vocal gift of the Spirit. This is generally accompanied by (at least) the first few sentences of the message the Lord desires them to speak. To receive and release the Spirit is a matter of faith. Galatians 3:5 says, "Therefore He who supplies the Spirit to you and works miracles among you, does He do it by the works of the law, or by the hearing of faith?" To prepare one's self to be used by the anointing is not a matter of the works of the law, nor is it the controlling religious mantra of "thou shalt not, taste not, touch not, handle not the things of the world." It is not the admiring of angels, nor any form of false humility in neglect of the body, thinking that self-inflicted suffering will gain "brownie points" with the Father.

Receiving the Spirit is the direct result of:
1. Knowing that God has given the Spirit as a free gift.
2. Knowing the free gift was purchased by the death of Christ, once and for all.
3. Knowing that God's Word is true, and God is true to His Word.
4. Knowing that the testimony of God is greater than the witness of man.
5. Knowing that even if the flesh says, "He is not here," the flesh is blind and knows nothing.
6. Knowing that because God has poured out His Spirit freely, He has to be here, just like water poured from a pitcher into a glass. Once you start pouring, it is in the glass. God has poured out His love and filled our hearts with the Holy Spirit.

Because all of the above are true, the Spirit is here, and like wind, cannot be still. It is always moving, and I can receive the knowledge of His moving presence and enjoy all the benefits of His wonderful anointing.

"For this reason I bow my knees to the Father of our Lord Jesus Christ, from whom the whole family in heaven and earth is named, that He would grant you, according to the riches of His glory, to be strengthened with might through His Spirit in the inner man, that Christ may dwell in your hearts through faith; that you, being rooted and grounded in love, may be able to comprehend with all the saints what is the width and length and depth and height to know the love of Christ which passes knowledge; that you may be filled with all the fullness of God." (Eph. 3:14-19)

Benefits of Receiving and Releasing the Anointing Power

"But ye shall receive power, after that the Holy Ghost is come upon you: and ye shall be witnesses unto me both in Jerusalem, and in all Judaea, and in Samaria, and unto the uttermost part of the earth." (Acts 1:8 KJV)

Examples of power being a benefit of the anointing can be seen in the lives of Samson and David. In the above verse and in many other places, in the N.T. the word *power* means "supernatural workings." Things are accomplished by a supernatural power, transcending time, space, matter and circumstance, literally sweeping them out of the way.

The Anointing Destroys the Yoke of Bondage

We all have bondages – habits, attitudes, fears, and emotions - that desperately need to be broken. The anointing (the Holy Spirit) brings freedom of spirit, soul, mind, and of understanding. Where the Spirit of the Lord is there is liberty (freedom).

"And it shall come to pass in that day, that his burden shall be taken away from off thy shoulder, and his yoke from off thy neck, and the yoke shall be destroyed because of the anointing." (Isa. 10:27 KJV)

The Anointing Teaches Us
"But the anointing which ye have received of him abideth in you, and ye need not that any man teach you: but as the same anointing teacheth you of all things..." (1 John 2:27 KJV)

"And I will pray the Father, and He shall give you another Comforter, that He may abide with you forever; Even the Spirit of truth; whom the world cannot receive, because it seeth Him not, neither knoweth Him: but ye know Him; for He dwelleth with you, and shall be in you. But the Comforter, which is the Holy Spirit, whom the Father will send in my name, He shall teach you all things..." (John 14:16, 17, 26 KJV)

The same anointing that sets us free will also give us knowledge. Knowledge not only makes freedom productive, it also prevents us from becoming entangled again in other bondages. Freedom can be intoxicating: most teenagers want freedom – freedom to test, to try, to see what's out there in the big world - but freedom without wisdom, knowledge and God's guidance can be the path to prison and destruction.

The Anointing Brings Change
When Samuel anointed Saul to be king of Israel, he said the Spirit of the Lord would come upon him, and he would prophesy and be turned into another man.

"After that you shall come to the hill of God where the Philistine garrison is. And it will happen, when you have come there to the city, that you will meet a group of prophets coming down from the high place with a stringed instrument, a tambourine, a flute, and a harp before them; and they will be prophesying. Then the Spirit of the Lord will come upon you, and you will prophesy with them and be turned into another man. And let it be, when these signs come to you, that you do as the occasion demands; for God is with you." (1 Sam. 10:5-7)

I know what you are saying right now. "How could this be? Saul was a man totally dominated by self, carnal appetites, and his own wisdom and desires." The prophet Samuel told him that the Spirit of the Lord would come upon him, and he would find himself saying things he had not planned to say. I've heard myself saying things I didn't plan to say because the Spirit of the Lord had come upon me. Occasionally, at the last minute I've changed my whole sermon as I walked up to the pulpit - even though I had studied for hours on the sermon in my hands - because the anointing rose up and showed me the sermon I'd planned to preach was either not appropriate for that time or place, or it was cultural tradition instead of the Word of the Lord. Not only did Samuel tell Saul that he would prophesy, he told him that he would be changed into another person. People throughout the Body of Christ are trying to change themselves and others. Change takes place as we present ourselves as living sacrifices to the Lord, and we let the anointing of His Spirit work in our lives.

The Anointing is Like the Name of the Lord Poured Forth

"...the name of the Lord is as ointment poured forth..." (Song of Songs 1:3).

ANOINTED TO ROAR

Oil is used throughout the Bible to symbolize the Holy Spirit. It also speaks of the anointing. The name of the Lord, then, is like the anointing poured forth. In the name of the Lord, we are delivered from evil. In the name of the Lord, we receive help in times of trouble. In the name of the Lord, we find comfort, encouragement, and strength. Not only are we to pray in the name of Jesus, but we will also accomplish great and wonderful works in His name.

When I look back at my life, I see a multitude of answered prayers and works of faith and power accomplished as the name of Jesus was poured forth in a mighty anointing. When I first began to preach, I went to the pulpit in the name of "I have graduated from Bible School." That lasted maybe a couple of Sundays. The following weeks, I tried to preach in the name of "I am the Senior Pastor, so listen to me." After those few hard-knock educational experiences, I realized I had nothing else to say and I was ready to quit. Then I learned to go to the pulpit and preach in the name of the Lord, and the words given to me by the anointing were like ointment being poured forth. My mind would become flooded with inspiring ideas, and my mouth would become filled with anointed words. People would say such things as "This is alive!" "This is fresh!" "This is real!" "This is relevant!" "This is wonderful!" I witnessed how a five-minute prophetic statement could have more effect than a two-hour sermon from procured theology.

About 25 years ago, while attending Bible college I found myself in a leadership class taught by my spiritual father, Pastor Glen Foster; a true prophetic roaring lion. When he opened his mouth to prophesy, his roar would wind up being heard from Arizona all across the nations. In this particular Bible college class I remember how he told of a very personal and miraculous testimony to all of us next-generation, prophetic, roaring lions (ministry leaders) that dramatically impacted my life to this day. The story goes as follows as was told in his own words:

> "When I was about twenty years old, I experienced an incident I will never forget. I was in an oil explosion. My car caught on fire, and the building filled with flames. Fire went into my mouth, up my nose, and burned off my eyebrows. I didn't have time to fast and pray or call for the elders of the church. Suddenly, from the depths of my spirit, and out of my mouth, came the words, 'Jesus save me!' The name of the Lord put out the fire in the building, and extinguished the pain in my body. Within a few hours, I had received total healing. When you need it, the name of the Lord, whether it is Jehovah Jireh, Jehovah Rophe, or the Lord My Banner, becomes like ointment poured out."

Unity Produces Greater Anointing

"Behold, how good and how pleasant it is for brethren to dwell together in unity! It is like the precious oil upon the head, running down on the beard, the beard of Aaron, Running down on the edge of his garments. It is like the dew of Hermon, Descending upon the mountains of Zion; for there the Lord commanded the blessing—Life forevermore." (Ps. 133)

The above Psalm illustrates the greater level of anointing that exists when brethren dwell together in unity. In a setting where brothers and sisters in Christ come together (and we all need to be in unity with someone), the anointing, like the precious oil that was poured upon Aaron, covers us from head to toe. The anointing we experience when we are gathered in unity doesn't just touch the forehead; it flows down through the hair, the garments, and drips on the feet so that we also walk in an anointing. We are completely covered by an anointing. If each believer is anointed, then it is only logical that the coming together of many anointed individuals creates an atmosphere where the Spirit of God can move in greater measure. This is called the corporate anointing. There is a greater level of anointing and power that is released when God's people agree in faith and are in one mind and in one accord with the promises and purpose of God. Every time we attend church, we place ourselves into a setting where we can both receive and release the anointing. Every time I go to church, I go out of the building feeling like the holy oil has been poured upon my head and is running down to my feet. I sense that something of God has been imparted into my spirit.

An impartation of anointing often comes through the prophetic word. This is another reason why it is important to attend church. When a minster steps up to the pulpit to preach, he or she should be stepping up to speak out (prophetically roar out) what secrets have been shown to him or her in the secret place of the Most High. When I step into the pulpit every week I come with a word from the Lord for the hour. I do not come with a half-baked, half cooked, sugar coated, make-you-feel-good sermonette. When I step behind the pulpit to preach, whether in my own church or as a guest-speaker elsewhere, I know that I have come with the Word of the Lord, because God instructed me what I am to say and preach. Just like my heavenly Father, the Lion of the tribe of Judah who has roared before me, the congregation recognizes that what I preach is the unadulterated, uncompromisable Word of the Lord. In what I preach, they sense God speaking directly to them, roaring truth into their lives. Every week after a service, people come up and tell me, "That word was just for me Pastor."

I say, "That is right, it was just for you." Another person says, "That word was just for me." I say, "You are right, that word was just for you also." Yet another says, "I don't see how that word could have fit anybody in this building like it fit me." I say, "God had me preach that word just for you." Still another will say, "Did you talk to my wife or husband about the conversation we just had in our house last night? It was like you were a fly on the wall listening to everything that was said." Some will say, "Pastor, you must have heard my prayers and agony at the altar of prayer. That word was just for me!" This is what happens when a prophetic word falls on the Body of Christ. The impartation of anointing breaks yokes, sets people free and brings understanding.

"If a trumpet is blown in a city, will not the people be afraid? If there is calamity in a city, will not the Lord have done it? Surely the Lord God does nothing, unless He reveals His secret to His servants the prophets. A lion has roared! Who will not fear? The Lord God has spoken! Who can but prophesy?" (Amos 3:6-8)

The anointing is also poured out by prayer and communion. In 1 Kings, Chapter 8, the people began to pray and dedicate the temple to the Lord. As they stood before Him in prayer, the glory cloud came down and filled the place with such a powerful manifestation of the presence of God that the priests could not even stand up to minister. They literally fell down under the power of God.

"And it came to pass, when the priests came out of the holy place, that the cloud filled the house of the Lord, so that the priests could not continue ministering because of the cloud; for the glory of the Lord filled the house of the Lord." (1 Kin. 8:10-11)

53

I received the anointing to preach in a young adults prayer meeting. There were just a few of us hungry, passionate, twenty something's trying to get in touch with God's plan and purpose for our lives. While gathered around a fireplace, there were five of us asking for God to place a fire within our hearts to do His will. Hour after hour passed by; I thought, "What am I doing here just staring into this fireplace? I should be going home soon. I don't care if they are having some of my favorite food and desserts afterward." Somehow I found the will to continue on in the prayer meeting. As I fought against a spirit of slumber and worked hard at staying engaged, at times I just sat in God's presence saying, "I bless you Lord. I love you, Lord. I praise you, Lord. I yield to you, and to your Spirit Lord." Then the breakthrough finally came! A burning glory entered the living room of that little prayer meeting and enveloped all five of us young adults. A divine anointing was placed upon us like hot, fiery coals from off the altar of heaven; like the coals that were placed by the seraphim on the lips of Isaiah the prophet long ago (Isa. 6:6-8). It was in that little obscure prayer meeting that I was anointed and empowered to do what I've been doing now for the past 32 years. But, it all began through *praying and waiting* on God for the anointing!

The Spirit of the Lord Rushed Upon David

The Spirit of the Lord came upon David when Samuel took the horn of oil and anointed him to be the next king. I Samuel 16:11 reads "...and Samuel said to Jesse, 'Send and bring him. For we will not sit down till he comes here.' So he sent and brought him in. Now he was ruddy, with bright eyes, and good-looking. And the Lord said, 'Arise, anoint him; for this is the one!' Then Samuel took the horn of oil and anointed him in the midst of his brothers; and the Spirit of the Lord came upon David from that day forward."

Over the years, as I have been given the invitation and opportunity to preach at revivals, healing services, conferences, and crusades here in the states and abroad, I have often felt the Spirit of the Lord rush upon me and the special anointing for that particular service takes me over. This rushing anointing has revealed wisdom, words of knowledge, hidden mysteries, doctrine, healings, and miracles to my spirit and then in the flow of the rushing I am able to just release them (roar them out) over the people. Over the years, I have learned to find peace and comfort knowing that when I arrive on the scene to any one of these particular meetings, it is not what I have come to say, bring, or offer, but it is the anointing that breaks every yoke and I am just a mere tool in releasing the rushing flow of the anointing. Whenever I preach, I wait for the anointing – the moving of the Holy Spirit. I refuse to speak or prophesy without the assuring manifested presence of God evidenced in a service. If it is not there I will not speak or give a 'Thus sayeth the Lord.' In fact, many times I do not have a full plan laid out six months in advance. At times this has even frustrated all the planners on my church staff; as they are constantly looking for me to give them a calendar in advance. I have told them over and over to please give me grace and to bear with me as I am constantly opening the windows of my spirit, waiting for the nudging, the leading, most of all the rushing wind of the Spirit. If the Spirit does not move, I just go to the pulpit and tell the people, "I am sorry but I don't have anything to say."

Just as the wind can beat on the outside of a building but not touch the occupants inside, it is also possible for the wind of the Spirit to be blowing and for us to keep our spiritual doors and windows closed. It is easy to become so taken up with the natural activities of life, that we lose conscious awareness of the ever-abiding presence of the Spirit, both within and without. We must choose to "leave our spiritual doors and windows open" and be sensitive to the flow of the Spirit of God. Sometimes, the wind blows hard enough to rattle the windows and get our attention; then we open the way and let the fresh gusts sweep through. Most of the time the wind of the Spirit is not harsh; instead, it is soft, gentle and quiet, waiting for us to open the doors and windows by faith to receive an adequate supply of the moving of the Spirit, according to our need. At times, a gentle gust through the curtains is enough to refresh the house, cool the environment, and create a beautiful atmosphere. At other times, we need to pull back the curtains, open all the windows and doors, and let the wind whip through the house unrestrained. We need the wind of the Spirit – the moving, flowing, penetrating, yoke-destroying, life-giving flow of the anointing, in one way or another every day of our lives. Whether the anointing is described as oil, water, fire, or rain, the principle is the same. We have to use our faith to release that which God has deposited in us. There is enough anointing stored up in all believers combined to break every yoke and set every captive free. But many Christians keep this wonderful anointing sealed up in their own private alabaster box. We can learn to be like the woman in Matthew 26:7, who broke her prized alabaster box and poured her precious ointment that filled the entire house with the sweet oil fragrance upon Jesus' feet. Our homes, churches, and communities can also be filled with the beautiful graces of the Holy Spirit. However, we need not break the box, for God has provided ways to release the Spirit that remains accessible to all believers. We can begin to release the flow of this great power, once we settle the fact that the Spirit is always present, around us and within us, to lead us and guide us.

THE EVER INCREASING GLORY

Ways In Which The Spirit Is Released:

The Spirit is released by Meditating on the Word

Like the breeze created from the revolving of a fan, the Spirit moves apathetic emotions and thoughts into a life-giving direction of joy, peace, love, hope, or numerous other expressions of divine life. King David, the anointed singer of Israel, said that meditating on the Word caused a fire to burn within his soul. Fire is a symbol of the moving of the Spirit. Fires cause drafts of air and temperature changes. All these sensations are descriptive of the effect of releasing the Spirit.

The Spirit is Released by Singing

The singing of hymns, worship choruses, and scripture songs release the Spirit within the one singing and in those who hear. The anointing upon music breaks yokes, destroys burdens, and lifts spirits. We have found that truths which are difficult to teach, and are often met with great resistance, are cheerfully received when they are introduced through singing and music. The anointing in the music makes it much easier to learn and accept these truths.

The Spirit is Released by Praying

There are many kinds of prayers which release the Spirit such as prayers of petition, prayers of fellowship, and prayers claiming one's rights. When we are petitioning, the Holy Spirit helps our weaknesses and teaches us how to pray, or He sometimes prays through us. This is especially true when we open all the windows and doors and let the Spirit blow through us, and we pray in our prayer languages. Oh, how the wind of the Spirit blows when we seek fellowship, and the fire of divine love burns in the fireplace of yielded hearts. I have, from time to time, met people coming from the place of prayer who were releasing the overflow, and it lifted my spirit. Oh, how the Spirit flashes with lightning, rolls with thunder, and stimulates the heart with confidence when our prayers become forceful and we begin to claim our rights. The Spirit yearns to be released into the dimension of the dynamics, the dunamis, of the delivering power of the miraculous. Mountains will be removed and rough places will be made smooth when the Spirit is released through a command or a demand while claiming our rights.

The Spirit is Released by Preaching

Anointed preaching, teaching, exhorting and testifying releases the Spirit. As He said, "Let the redeemed of the Lord say so..." (Ps. 107:2). Again, He said, "And they overcame him by the blood of the Lamb and by the word of their testimony..." (Rev. 12:11). Even the second greatest preacher known in the Bible (right next to Jesus Himself) the Apostle Paul declared of his preaching in 1 Corinthians 2:1-5; "And I, brethren, when I came to you, did not come with excellence of speech or of wisdom declaring to you the testimony of God. For I determined not to know anything among you except Jesus Christ and Him crucified. I was with you in weakness, in fear, and in much trembling. And my speech and my preaching were not with persuasive words of human wisdom, but in demonstration of the Spirit and of power, that your faith should not be in the wisdom of men but in the power of God."

The Spirit is Released by Resting in Faith

Psalm 46:10 says, "Be still and know that I am God." Hebrews 4:10 says, "For he who has entered His rest has himself also ceased from his works as God did from His." Resting (by faith) in God's finished works releases the Spirit. We have so often cried out to God for help, and the answer has come back, "Wait.

58

Be patient. Only believe. Trust in quietness and confidence. Be anxious for nothing, but in everything by prayer and supplication, with thanksgiving, let your requests be made known to God; and the peace of God, which surpasses all understanding, will guard your hearts and minds through Christ Jesus." (Phil. 4:6-7)

The Spirit has spoken to us so often, "You need not fight this battle; hold your peace, for the battle is the Lord's." Whenever we step into our appointed place and let God be God, we release the Spirit to be our comforter, our guide and our shield. He becomes the one who goes before us, the wind that lifts our wings, the breath that gives us life, and the fire that keeps us warm. We experience the knowledge of the presence of the Holy One of Israel who is our shield, our rock, our fortress, and our rear guard. The Holy Spirit is more eager to move through the open doors and windows of our lives than we have realized. We will learn to appreciate this truth more and more as we experience the simplicity of releasing the Spirit. We can release the Spirit by singing when we feel bad and by giving thanks even when we feel helpless and hopeless. We can release the Spirit in a powerful way when we have been wronged and return good for evil. We never again need to say, "If the Spirit would only move," or "Someday, when the Spirit moves again." But we can release the Spirit at anytime and say, "I can do all things through Christ [the Anointed One – who lives in me and] who strengthens me." (Phil. 4:13)

Since all believers have received the same general anointing, all may participate in the release of the Spirit without further qualifications of a works system or an ordination of an ecclesiastical system. We do not have to send a telegram to headquarters asking permission for the Spirit to move. The release of the Spirit is based solely upon our personal relationship with the Holy Spirit Himself, so all we have to do is whisper His name in faith, for His name is as ointment poured forth. It is no wonder then that the Apostle Paul said in Colossians 3:17, "And whatever you do in word or deed, do all in the name of the Lord Jesus, giving thanks to God the Father through Him." He further clarified in Romans 15:17-19, "Therefore I have reason to glory in Christ Jesus in the things which pertain to God. For I will not dare to speak of any of those things which Christ has not accomplished through me, in word and deed, to make the gentiles obedient— in mighty signs and wonders, by the power of the Spirit of God..."

Chapter 5
The Power of Aaron's Anointing

As we study the Psalm 133 anointing in Aaron's life, we want to focus on the factors that held the anointing steady for so many years. Aaron was anointed after the Israelites were brought up out of Egypt, and for the rest of his life he walked in that anointing. Have you ever wished you could go deeper with God? The Aaronic anointing is an anointing that goes deeper than the average person realizes is possible. After you are born again, you are still not satisfied; you want more. After you receive the baptism of the Holy Spirit and other wonderful works of God, you still want to go deeper, beyond the veil. The veil will remain until our hearts fully turn to Christ. The Aaronic anointing takes us into the Holiest of Holies. God is calling for a generation to receive Aaron's anointing, to go beyond the veil, to behold the hidden deeper things of God. This generation is called the *enlightened* or *educated* generation, yet there are some things that God still has hidden from us. God still has some mysteries that we can only comprehend by the Aaronic anointing. So it is important to look into those mysteries.

Psalm 133:1 NKJV, "Behold how good and how pleasant it is for brethren to dwell together in unity!" Aaron walked in unity, in humility as a servant, and in the revealed Word of the Lord through Moses. How beautiful it is for brethren to dwell in unity. It is like the precious oil upon the head, or the anointing, running down on the beard of Aaron, running down to the edge or to the hem of his garment.

Aaron Walked in Unity

God hates the sowing of division among the brethren. Sowing division strikes at unity and cuts away at the very source from which the body of Christ receives its life. Sowing division blocks the flow of God's power to do His will in individuals, families, and communities. The full blessings of God cannot be received when there is no unity. The Apostle Paul spoke about this in Ephesians 4:1-3, "I, therefore, the prisoner of the Lord, beseech you to walk worthy of the calling with which you were called, with all lowliness and gentleness, with longsuffering, bearing with one another in love, endeavoring to keep the unity of the Spirit in the bond of peace."

Sometimes, division is sown because of your own inner heartaches, jealousy and judgments - creating so much inner pressure to your emotions that you fail to control your tongue. It is so easy to slip into this kind of negative attitude. My church knows that I have coined a phrase for this inner pressure that we all fall subject to from time to time. I call it a "Baditude." Sometimes it's because of someone else's heartaches or because of your strong sympathetic feelings for a friend or family member. Sometimes it's because of someone's un-sympathetic feelings toward you. Whatever the cause might be, we still have to work at keeping unity within the body of Christ. Nothing could separate Aaron from Moses permanently in their ministry together. The anointing always broke the yoke and brought them back into one accord. However, there was a brief moment in Pastor Moses' ministry life that a "baditude" (the inner pressure) got to two of Moses' closest leaders and confidants; Miriam and Aaron. Both Miriam and Aaron's "baditudes" were driven by the inner pressure of personal judgments and a critical spirit towards a woman of color (a black woman), Moses' love interest and "First Lady" of the church (the Senior Pastors wife). It tried to breakdown and destroy their unity, power, and anointing in their ministry, as well as cause a church split in the Children of Israel Community Church. Let's take a quick look at this account in scripture:

Numbers 12:1-10, "Then Miriam and Aaron spoke against Moses because of the Ethiopian woman whom he had married; for he had married an Ethiopian woman. So they said, 'Has the Lord indeed spoken only through Moses? Has He not spoken through us also?' And the Lord heard it. (Now the man Moses was very humble, more than all men who were on the face of the earth.) Suddenly the Lord said to Moses, Aaron, and Miriam, 'Come out, you three, to the tabernacle of meeting!' So the three came out. Then the Lord came down in the pillar of cloud and stood in the door of the tabernacle, and called Aaron and Miriam. And they both went forward. Then He said, 'Hear now My words: If there is a prophet among you, I, the Lord, make Myself known to him in a vision; I speak to him in a dream. Not so with My servant Moses; He is faithful in all My house. I speak with him face to face, even plainly, and not in dark sayings; and he sees the form of the Lord. Why then were you not afraid to speak against My servant Moses?' So the anger of the Lord was aroused against them, and He departed. And when the cloud departed from above the tabernacle, suddenly Miriam became leprous, as white as snow. Then Aaron turned toward Miriam, and there she was, a leper."

God said to Aaron and Miriam, "I speak with Moses differently than I speak with you." We could liken this to the Word of God. The Word of God speaks, and that is what makes the difference in our lives. God does not normally speak to us audibly today (however He can if He chooses to do so). He speaks to us by His Spirit, comparable to what Elijah experienced as the "still small voice" (see I Kings 19:12). There is never a word that comes to us personally as individuals that is equal to the words of the Holy Bible. We must stay in the Bible and cleave to its words. We must watch for anything – any opinion, experience, feeling, outlook, or viewpoint – that would or could create a wedge. We must always see the O.T. through the N.T. and understand the N.T. through the O.T. God has bound them together; they are inseparable. The Word of God is not "Old" or "New". The Word of God is complete, lacking nothing and lives and abides forevermore! The person who lives in accordance with the Word will have a deeper anointing than the person who does not. Every now and then I come across scriptures that pierce my very soul. At that moment, I have a choice; to either close my eyes and slam the door shut on the Word, or to open the eyes of my heart and let His Word in and accept its truth.

When I first began trying to understand the promise of healing in the Word of God, the Holy Spirit had directed me to read books of other minister's experiences with the Lord in this area. There are scripture references in T.L. Osborne's books and teachings that absolutely altered my viewpoint on healing in our current times. It was like he reached out of the pages of his book with a club and knocked me over the head with it. One thing he said that deeply disturbed me was: "If God said you're healed and you believe you're healed, then you are healed. If you are healed, then quit whimpering and whining about how bad you feel and get up and start talking about what God has done for you." Finally, after much struggle, I made the decision to walk in unity with the Word, based upon this premise: "If the written Word says it, I believe it." When I said what the written Word said and walked in the way the written Word said to walk, my healing began to manifest. The many healings I have received are not because I'm special, but because I walk in unity with the written Word in thought, belief, attitude and confession. I continue to walk believing God knows what He is talking about.

Aaron Stayed in Unity

God told Aaron to join Moses in the wilderness. It is usually a wilderness experience that brings about a division in our relationship with God, or with our teachers and mentors. Generally, until we go into the wilderness for the first time, we listen to everything the preacher says, and we hang on to every word of God. We say, "Your will Lord, your will." When volunteers are needed, our hand is the first one to go up. We're the first one to the altar, but when God sends us into the wilderness, we start saying, "No Lord, I don't like this, I don't like that teaching. I don't know what has happened to my sweet church. I don't know what has happened to my kind pastor. It seems there are more thorns in his messages now than there are apple trees to sit under." Aaron went to the wilderness and joined himself to Moses. Not knowing what the outcome would be, he still endeavored to keep that unity of the Spirit. Then God said to Moses, "Go before the congregation, and begin to witness before them of what I am doing." It is one thing to be in the body and to be a partaker of what God is doing, but it is another thing to go before the body and be put under the microscope or on the inspection table and have your life judged, your witness proven, and your testimony considered. At that point, many will refuse to prophesy or to reveal their visions during the church services because they do not want everyone, especially the pastor, to hear and possibly judge what they say, but they will prophesy in small groups. They won't minister in cooperation with the whole body, but a time comes when God says, "You can't always hide in a corner. Submit your life before the body." That is when some people jump ship and run off to another church. You must stay in unity with God's purpose. Iron sharpens iron and during this sharpening process, you reach a point where you have to accept the fact that a person in the body who agitates you is actually being used of the Lord to help buffet, polish and perfect you.

Over the years I have been accused of being too soft on people and not holding them accountable. I have had people tell me that every time they see a problem, it appears to them that I turn my back and don't care to deal with it. I have learned that the congregation must be dealt with by not only the Senior Pastor's apostolic rod of instruction and correction, but also by other members of the congregation as well. We must learn how to bear one another's burdens, caring for one another, and sharing one another's sorrows and do it all in long-suffering. I have learned to be concerned with the cause of a person's pain instead of being concerned about their pain itself, or being too worried about the current "pain in the fanny" the person is causing me as their pastor at the moment. The pain of the children of Israel was a fear of being in bondage forever. They said, "Show us a miracle", but, on the other hand, they said, "Quit doing miracles because you are making things worse." Then, and now, the congregation remains unsatisfied with God (from a natural standpoint) but you can't use dissatisfaction as an excuse for self-serving. Have you ever been in a place in life where you could do whatever you wanted to do for a period of time? Most of us have. Did that really satisfy you? No. You just kept jumping from one thing to another until you finally said, "Forget it... I'll never be happy in this world!"

God said to Moses and Aaron in Exodus 9:1; "…go into Pharaoh and tell him, 'Thus says the Lord God of the Hebrews: 'Let My people go, that they may serve Me." Going before Pharaoh is a type of a confrontation with the devil that you (along with every other believer) must experience in order to find out:

1. How much power you have in God over the enemy and over what is still holding you captive and keeping you in bondage
    AND
2. How much carnality you still have in you. For example, the devil comes with fear, and you discover fears that you never realized before. Or you thought that you secured the victory over certain fears and you quickly realize by your response and by the devil's threats that your fears are still there.

Be assured that the devil will come. He is the Pharaoh, the force of captivity, the enforcer of bondage, and the seducer that tells you, "It is better to be in Goshen in bondage than to be out in the wilderness and have to become a soldier in order to get into the Promised Land." All of these facts teach us the need to exercise our authority over the devil. Some people attend church not because they are interested in hearing the Word of God, but to fulfill a religious obligation. In fact, they are offended by the Word when it starts cutting and dealing with them. God intentionally sets up circumstances to test our faith. These circumstances bring us to places where we confront fear, oppression, and criticism. I have stood before the devil and his criticism of me and my life while he brings them all up to the surface. When you stand before Pharaoh (the oppressor – the devil), all your flaws will come out and stand visible, because he is ruthless, unmerciful, inconsiderate, and he goes for the jugular vein every time. He will find your weakness, then he will exploit it and use it to get you out of unity with God, His Word, and His plan for your life.

I have had weeks when it felt as if I had lost the flow of the anointing because I got out of unity with God and His Word. I started to agree with Pharaoh (the devil) and his criticisms. I was held captive and oppressed by Pharaoh - believing there was no strength to remedy the weaknesses that was being exploited about me by my captor. When I did not walk in unity with God, I could not walk in the Lion's anointing. I had no powerful lion roar. All I could do was whimper like a frightened little mouse. Then I discovered something life changing in the scriptures that the Apostle Paul had written concerning his own struggles and weakness. In 2 Corinthians, Chapter 12, he described the Lord bringing perfect strength in the middle of his greatest weaknesses.

"And He said to me, "My grace is sufficient for you, for My strength is made perfect in weakness." Therefore most gladly I will rather boast in my infirmities, that the power of Christ may rest upon me. Therefore I take pleasure in infirmities, in reproaches, in needs, in persecutions, in distresses, for Christ's sake. For when I am weak, then I am strong." (2 Cor. 12:9-10)

Aaron Walked in Humility

Aaron also walked in humility in the role of a servant. When we first get saved, we are willing to do anything, such as sweep the floor, pick up trash, or run errands for the preacher and so on. New Christians are always thrilled that God would call them by name and ask them to do something. They feel good at the time, until later when they find that the Lord is calling them to a life of submission, servant-hood, and sacrifice. Everyone in the body of Christ – from the apostles through all the giftings, helps and members – are called to be servants. To be in a supportive role to Jesus Christ, one must stay straight, pure, and in power. He is the head, the Lord, the Chief in charge, the first and the last. We all operate in supportive roles, but we all have a tendency to come to the place where we want "my will, not thy will." When we first ran into His will, it was so great, and pure, so exciting, until He said, "Go clean up the mess you made." We protest, "But Lord, You always cleaned up my messes in the past." He brings us to a place of learning to walk in responsibility with a servant's heart. Most people who go wrong do so by going into self-exaltation. They become puffed up in their own minds. This was the same self-exalting fault of Lucifer. He wanted to place himself in the ruling seat of authority, but the reality was that in all his splendor, beauty and gifting he "puffed up" and wanted to be God. He wanted to share in the same omnipotent, unlimited, ruling power and authority as God. The reality was that he was just created to uplift, serve, and praise the God of all authority and unlimited power.

Many young Christians and inexperienced ministers, in their zeal to serve and be used of God, want important positions and titles rather than reality. That is the reason why I have no interest in fancy titles as prophet or apostle. I'm only interested in being known as a man after God's own heart, in being real, genuine, sincere, and letting the Holy Spirit move through me. When I do so, then it can only be said that it is the Lord who is at work in the midst of His people. God told Aaron that he would not be in charge, he would be following orders. People throughout the body of Christ are complaining that the Senior Pastor acts like a lord or a boss. Someone does have to be in charge, whether it is in the church house, the court house, the white house, the workplace, the home place, or in any other setting. The head leader in the local church is the Senior Pastor. Then, under the

Pastor, there are leaders in other departments, such as the Elders, Deacons, Associate Pastor, Minister of Music, the Youth Pastor, the Director for the Children's Education Department, etc. Those who work in those respective departments must learn to work with and alongside the leader in charge to eradicate chaos and breed excellence and vision in the House of God. The only one who is to be highly exalted and elevated is God Himself.

You can observe the anointing at work in the lives of people when it comes to them getting into the deeper things of God; their relationship and unity with God and with the Senior Pastor or the local church is stronger. Today, you can find people peddling all kinds of "deeper revelations" and "prophetic mysteries" that are not scripturally sound, and they do not promote spiritual health in the hearts of their listeners. These scripturally unsound visions come forth from the lips of those who are not willing to submit to proper fivefold authority and take sound direction, orders, or advice when they come into a city. They come from those who do not want to ask the local pastors what is going on in their city, and who do not ask them how they can work in unity with the local pastors. These glory peddlers often present themselves as greater than the local churches, and that their ministry provides better results that no other ministry can provide. The truth is, if the ministry is Christ's ministry, it can be found in any church, in that city. Regardless of the name of the church, when people get into unity with God, those participating can become useful vessels through whom God can do anything He pleases.

So many of us, when we start ministering in the gifts of the Spirit, become know-it-alls, not realizing that all the gifts of the Spirit are like meals taken by waiters and ministered to the hungry. This truth is illustrated in the feeding of the five thousand (John 6:4-14). Jesus gave the bread to each of His disciples. They, in turn, ministered it to the hungry. The disciples were never owners of the bread; they were only distributors of it. Yes, there were twelve baskets left over, enough for the disciples to have lunch for several days after they had returned home. This illustrates how we receive miracles while worshipping with the congregation, and then carry them to our household where we minister them once again. We should never exalt ourselves to the level of ownership, but we should consider ourselves as the Master's servants working together with God, ministering the blessings of the Kingdom and distributing the blessings abroad. If you went into a restaurant, sat down at a table, and the waitress or waiter began to tell you what to order and what to eat first, you would say, "Who do you think you are? I thought you were supposed to serve me." Aaron was able to remain in the role of a servant - everything he did was supportive. It is strange how some people want the church to support them, but they don't want to support the church. When they are in financial difficulty, they want the church to pay their bills and when they are financially solvent again, they don't want to tithe. That is a self-serving, humanistic viewpoint. Even people who say they don't believe in tithing should understand that if we are not supporting, we are just taking. If you are not a tither, you can fast and pray, but you will not get the Aaronic anointing until you become a supportive person. It is like prayer night; the number of people who support their churches on prayer nights are a minority. Some will never get the anointing they are looking for – regardless of how many prayer nights or Bible College classes they attend – until they are willing to support their local church.

Aaron adopted the heart of a servant even though he was called to be a leader. He was the first man to stand before the Holiest of Holies with the blood and with the glory of the Lord upon the altar. No one else walked in his footsteps until many years later. Though Aaron's anointing was a rare anointing, it can be ours today. "How", you ask? By learning to walk in humility and with a servant's heart. Not wanting to give orders, not coming to church saying, "Well, that preacher better preach on this…and they better not go overtime in the song service…if they start singing some of those older songs and hymns, I'm just going to go to church somewhere else!" The truth is, if you are going to come as a servant, you will say, "When there are older songs and hymns, I will rejoice in them – the anointing is here." When there are newer choruses that we may not know by heart, we can close our eyes and raise our hands. The anointing is still here, even if we can't sing them that well. If you take persecution humbly, the spirit of grace and glory will rest upon you. When things don't go your way in the church, we should endeavor to keep the unity of the Spirit and walk as a servant and say, "How can I help this go forward more effectively than it is instead of finding fault? Fault finding is part of my old nature. Being supportive is part of my new nature. I will choose to be supportive and let the anointing flow in my life." I guarantee you, as long as you walk with a humble heart, you will have an ever increasing lion's anointing in your life.

Finally, in walking in a supportive role, Aaron bore the reproaches of others. Romans 15:1-2 says, "We then who are strong ought to bear with the scruples of the weak, and not to please ourselves. Let each of us please his neighbor for his good, leading to edification." Romans 15:3 and Psalm 69:9 say, "The reproaches of those who reproached You fell on Me." Aaron, as a servant, let the reproaches fall on him. In fact, when Aaron went before the Lord, he carried the breastplate with the twelve stones, which represented all of Israel. In the O.T., guilt was transferred from one to another, from the people to the priest, and from the priest to the sacrifice. That is why today we glory in the cross. All our sins were transferred and nailed to it. Jesus transferred the reproach of the sins of the whole world onto His own body. The priest would then take the blood of the atoning lamb and go into the Holiest of Holies, and there obtain life, and that more abundantly, for the people. Aaron went into the Holiest of Holies once each year. When he came out, he had a New Year's decree of blessings and abundant life. Aaron's anointing causes a continually precious and beautiful flow of the administration of the government of God upon the household of faith. Instead of stumbling in the darkness of condemnation and guilt for weeks, months and years, we can cast our cares on Him on a daily basis just as we have been instructed. So, everyday we go into the Holiest of Holies and come out loaded with blessings. God said to Aaron, "Bear it. Care about it. Bring it to Me. Let the reproaches fall on thee."

2 Corinthians 5:18-19 tells us that God has given us the word of reconciliation and the ministry of reconciliation "...not imputing unto them their trespasses...," but instead saying, "I will cast them on Him because He cares for you." Many of you are in a position where you realize that is beginning to happen in your life. Instead of griping and complaining to people, you must realize that God has placed you where you can listen to people and minister the word of reconciliation unto them. This is a ministry that you must take seriously.

Aaron Walked in the Word of Moses

Aaron walked in the word of Moses in the same way that Jesus later walked in the word of His Father in heaven. Jesus said, "I do not speak My own words. I speak what the Father says to Me." (John 14:10-11) Moses had said to God, "I cannot speak to the people." God said, "I will give you the word and you give the word to Aaron. Aaron will speak as your mouth and you will speak as My mouth." (Ex. 7:1-2)

Let's get real here; it takes a tremendous amount of humility to be the second-hand mouthpiece for God. Aaron was humble and in unity with God, with His purposes, and with his Senior Pastor, Moses. The position most people like to be in is one where they can say, "I got the word and the confirmation; I hold the rod that budded AND I carry the people's trust!" The rod that budded was Moses' rod at first. He threw it down when confronting Pharaoh's magicians and it became a rod of miracles. When he picked it up, it was still a rod of miracles, but in time God said to Moses, "Give the rod to Aaron." You, like Aaron, must go through stages of growth in your walk with God and in your ministry development. Truths of the scripture are being revealed to you that will bring you from point A to point Z, bringing you to a fuller maturity. If you will walk as Aaron walked and say what the Word says, you will walk in the anointing of Aaron. Every step of the way, God will be teaching you through the truths that will come alive through teaching from the pulpit, through reading the Word, attending Bible college classes, listening to inspired spirit-filled messages via television, radio, CD's, podcasts over the internet..., etc. Key scriptures will come to you in your dreams, while you are sitting at the table and on your way to work. They will begin to challenge and illuminate areas of your life, and lead you on from glory to glory. In order for you to go on from glory to glory, you must come to the place where you will say what the Word says, regardless of your circumstances or how you feel.

When Pharaoh would say, "What about this or that?" Or when the people of Israel would say, "What about this or that?" Aaron's response was, "Well, God said to Moses..." I am sure people came to Aaron and said, "Don't you have any other opinions for us? Don't you have eyes? Why don't you tell us what you see? Don't you have ears? Doesn't God ever speak to you?" Aaron had no revelations, no words, and no authority of his own. The authority of his anointing was that he should only say what Moses said; His authority rested strictly in Moses. Our Moses today is the Bible. We become an Aaron whenever we say what the Bible says. That is what gave Aaron the authority to go in before the mercy seat - it wasn't just his special garments. A priest could wear the proper garments and still not be walking in unity, supportive humility, or in the word of Moses. A priest who was not walking in divine order would be struck dead when the manifested glory of God came upon the mercy seat. Even the mercy seat can be a deadly place for a person who is walking in rebellion. You may ask, "How can that be possible? It seems to be a contradiction." It is only possible when you can understand that flesh cannot live in the unveiled glory of God. In order to be released from fleshly ways, you must get into the Spirit and into Aaron's anointing. Aaron's anointing compels you to give up on your own wisdom and authority. You have to lean on God and say, "God, I can't do this on my own."

We can live in peace and confidence because we know there is divine power in the Aaronic anointing that will take us beyond every conflict, strife, and struggle. It will bring us into revelations of light that will illuminate the dark places. In the latter part of 2013 to early 2014, a great prophecy came forth that said, "Every year of this decade will be a new beginning. I am giving you ten years of new beginnings." In this next ten years, there will be an explosion in this new course of history. Many people are going to come into the house of God with the Aaronic anointing. These will walk in unity, humility and support; they will walk in the Word of the Lord. If God said it, receive it, (that settles it!) and believe it until you see it!

I am getting old enough now to dream such wonderful dreams and wise enough to lead a people into greater possibilities. When God raised up our Desert Rose Community Church congregation and our Gateway International Bible College, He said, "I'm going to give you hundreds of pillars." I know that is the Aaronic anointing that makes these pillars. God will give us hundreds of people who will endeavor to stay together in unity, who will continue to be servants through thick and thin, who will walk in the vision and in the Word of the Lord regardless of circumstances. God said, "When I get these pillars in place, this city will be swept into the Kingdom of God, from border to border." God is not just building up pillars in our church – He is building up pillars in every church that will hear the voice of the Lord. What God is saying to one church, He is saying to every church. He may use different terminology, different typology or methodology of dealing with His people, but the results will be the same from His eternal point of view. When the Lion of Judah roars, all His prophetic people will hear it like a grand shofar and come running to fulfill His kingdom purposes.

"Will a lion roar in the forest, when he has no prey? Will a young lion cry out of his den, if he has caught nothing? If a trumpet is blown in a city, will not the people be afraid? Surely the Lord God does nothing, unless He reveals His secret to His servants the prophets. A lion has roared! Who will not fear? The Lord God has spoken! Who can but prophesy?" (Amos 3:4, 6-8,)

Chapter 6
The Five-Fold Anointing of David's Strength

King David's life and ministry illustrates how effective the anointing can be. The anointing (the supernatural power of God) worked in David's life from his childhood to old age, from caring for his father's sheep, to his victory over Goliath. Every battle David fought, he won by the power of the anointing in his life. This anointing working in David's life is illustrated in 1 Samuel 17:34-37, where he killed a lion and a bear, and all through the books of Samuel, where he and his army slew thousands in battle with a sword. What was the source of David's strength that enabled him to be victorious in all these things? You can discover the source of his great strength by exploring the account of his life. Once you discover what that source is, you will also be able to live a victorious Christian life like David. You can read many accounts in David's life of him singing, dancing, praising God, and being a man after God's own heart. You may have even sang the song, "When the Spirit of the Lord moves in my heart, I will sing like David sang...I will dance like David danced...I will praise like David praised." But there is something very important you must do. You must put your mind where your mouth is and live the victorious life David lived. You must be a man (or woman) after God's own heart. When you are, you will actually be able to sing, dance and praise God with the anointing David had.

1 Samuel 25:29 KJV says, "...but the soul (life) of my lord (speaking of David) shall be bound in the bundle of life with the Lord thy God..." The N.T. equivalent of this verse is Colossians 3:3, "...and your life is hid with Christ in God." In the original language, "...the bundle of life..." was a little pouch in which people carried all their valuables. The valuables we carry in our bundle of life are the riches of God. The riches of God are being bound around you and your life is being bound up (hidden) in Jesus Christ. This mystery of being "hidden" or bound up in Jesus Christ is the source of your strength to live the victorious Christian life. You might ask, "How can I live a victorious Christian life when I have such a hard time trying not to sin?" Well, sin can be overcome, however, there is one very important thing that one must possess in order for this to be accomplished. This one necessary thing is to have the strength that is in Christ.

One challenge numerous people struggle with overcoming is depression. It is so difficult for some people to overcome that they go to the extreme of just giving up and make the confession that there is no possible way for them to cease from being depressed. But, just as we can be delivered from sin, we can also be delivered from the adversity of depression. This deliverance from depression comes through the strength and power of the anointing, which is in "the bundle of life with the Lord your God." There are some special verses found in Psalm 18 that you should underline when you study that chapter. I highly recommend that you study it often. If you study it, and underline these special verses, they might just jump out at you everytime you need them. These verses reveal the source of David's great strength, and how he was able to accomplish all the things he did.

THE FIVE FOLD ANOINTING OF DAVID'S STRENGTH

Psalm 18:28 KJV says, "For thou wilt light my candle (lamp): the Lord my God will enlighten my darkness." Your candle (or lamp) is your spirit, which He lights, or enlightens by the power of the anointing. The anointing will remove the darkness by which your life is shrouded, regardless of the depths of that darkness. God promises that He will give light to your candle. Your candle (spirit) will be so enlightened by the light of the Lord burning within it; that ALL of your darkness will ultimately be illuminated.

"For by thee I have run through a troop; and by my God have I leaped over a wall." (Psalm 18:29 KJV)

"It is God who girdeth me with strength, and maketh my way perfect." (Psalm 18:32 KJV)

The strength David was empowered with came from the Lord. Psalm 18:35 KJV says, "Thou has also given me the shield of thy salvation: and thy right hand hath holden me up…"

Psalm 18:37-38 KJV reads, "I have pursued mine enemies, and overtaken them: neither did I turn again till they were consumed. I have wounded them that they were not able to rise: they are fallen under my feet." This illustrates how broad or how great this anointing can be in a person's life.

Psalm 18:39-40 KJV describes the extent of the strength we receive. "For thou hast girded me with strength unto the battle: thou hast subdued under me those that rose up against me. Thou hast also given me the necks of mine enemies: that I might destroy them that hate me."

It is said of Martin Luther that he threw a bottle of ink at the devil. The devil, as everyone knows, could not be hit by a bottle of ink, so the bottle broke and the ink splashed and ran down the wall. When Martin Luther saw the ink running down the wall and being wasted, the Lord showed him that instead of throwing bottles of ink at the devil, he should use the ink to write the Word of God on paper. The Word of God written on paper would destroy the devil when it got into the people's minds and down into their hearts. Having the Word of God in our mind is the proper way to take hold of the neck of our enemy. I have seen people who, when praying, reach out at the devil and roar, "I've got you devil and I'm going to shake you to death!" After they left that wonderful, enthusiastic prayer time, they had nothing to stand on because they had no Word of God in their mind. The way to get the neck of your enemy is to get knowledge, wisdom, and understanding. This will give you the ability to stand in the truth.

"For You have armed me with strength for the battle; You have subdued under me those who rose up against me. You have also given me the necks of my enemies, So that I destroyed those who hated me. They cried out, but there was none to save; even to the Lord, but He did not answer them. Then I beat them as fine as the dust before the wind; I cast them out like dirt in the streets." (Ps. 18:39-42)

At times, we may get so angry with the enemy that we feel like stomping, but the enemy cannot be cast out by physical activity. The only way to cast out the enemy like dirt under our feet is by keeping our minds fixed on the Lord. We disregard the enemy's lies, his attacks and his threats that our doom is imminent; they do not influence us at all. We are not influenced by lies. In fact, when the devil speaks a lie, he is speaking of himself. When the enemy speaks of your doom being near, it is actually his doom that is near in the areas where he had you hemmed in.

Important points concerning the fivefold anointing of David:

The Battle is the Lord's

David saw that the battle was not against him, but against the Lord (1 Sam. 17:47). The enemy has no real concern at all about us; his concern is with God. It is God who he wants to hurt. The reason he fights us – the reason the circumstances of life are set against us – is not because we have something credible of ourselves, we are just earthen vessels. The wrath of the devil is focused against the Christ in us. This truth is also illustrated in the life of Joseph. Joseph saw this truth when his brothers tried to kill him. Instead of Joseph hating his brothers for what they had attempted to do, he recognized that they did what they did because he had a treasure. Joseph had visions and dreams; he had a destiny. God had revealed to Joseph His purposes for his life. It was the fulfillment of these purposes that the devil was trying to destroy because he knew that it wouldn't just impact his own life, but Joseph's destiny would impact the entire world and the world to come. Both David and Joseph began to learn at early ages. Both men endured rejection, hostility, and conflict from those they loved, even violence from their own brothers. They realized their calling in life was not to win the approval of their brothers - who were trying to become something in the flesh. Neither David nor Joseph sought to follow their brother's examples. Their calling was to follow God and be accepted by Him. Later, in the N.T., Jesus said to those who were struggling with faith, "How can you believe, who receive honor from one another, and do not seek the honor that comes from the only God?" (John 5:44)

1 Samuel 25 tells the story of David and the evil, surly man named Nabal and his beautiful, intelligent wife, Abigail. Nabal had refused to give provisions to David and his men when they were in the wilderness, even when their presence had been a protection for Nabal's herds and flocks. Because of this, David was determined to kill Nabal, but Nabal's wife, Abigail, intervened and took food to David and his men. When she met David on the way, she said, "Don't do this. The battle is the Lord's battle. Nabal is a fool; he doesn't hate you because you are David or because you are a Jew. He hates you because of your God. He is the son of the devil and he is fighting the God of salvation. So put up your sword, David, and don't fight your own battles. Retreat and rest in the Lord, and glorify Him. He will find a reason to bless and honor you above what otherwise would have been impossible." Abigail's words were recognized by David as being filled with wisdom, so he blessed her and told her that God had sent her to keep him from shedding blood. David turned the matter over to the Lord and in ten days (the number of dominion), Nabal was dead. David was not defensive. He was not going to attempt to fight his own battle. When we learn to stop fighting our own battles and learn to quit being defensive, God will move on our behalf.

In order to get our minds straight, a few things are required:
1. Prayer
2. Self-denial or Denial of Self-will
3. Meditation upon the Word of God

God has a place where He has hidden all the treasures of wisdom and knowledge. These are hidden in Jesus Christ. Our lives are to be bound up in Him.

The battle is the Lord's. Sometimes the devil tries to get us off track by placing us at odds with someone, but we are not to wrestle against flesh and blood. Why? Because the battle is the Lord's. Many Christians are blind to this fact, and the devil just sits back and laughs at their blind beliefs. They think that they can fight their own battles with their weapons of cynicism, quarreling, name-calling, shunning, and division. All these weapons actually stop the flow of the Spirit. There is only one way. None of the other methods, such as one believer trying to manipulate others for their personal benefit will work. The one and only way that warfare will work, is the mind of Christ must settle into our mind and convince us that 'His Word' is true, just, righteous, and the only way. When we try to fight with these weapons that stop the flow of the spirit, we are magnifying the enemy. David did not want to magnify the enemy, instead, he wanted to magnify the Lord. If we magnify the enemy, our problems will get bigger and bigger. If we magnify the Lord, our problems will get smaller and smaller. If you want to have smaller problems, magnify the Lord. David learned to have a big God and a little problem. When God gets bigger in your eyes, your problems will always get smaller.

We have two different responses to the problems we face:
1. To become defensive
2. To surrender in faith and hope

We can learn to bind our souls with the truth that the anointing always teaches us that there is nothing that we cannot overcome.

Overcoming is "laying down your life". Our prayer, then, should be, "Lord, I lay down my life." God is trying to do something in us and that is what the battle is about. The call of Christianity is that we are to lay down our lives. This is the meaning behind learning to lay down your sword and letting God fight the battle. He will fight the battle for you when you get to the place where you can't bear it, handle it or change it. Then, lay down your life and say, "Lord, I die!" After that moment, you will be resurrected to a new life – a new life in which you will live and move in the life and strength of the Lord. You die so that He might live. John 3:30 says, "He must increase, but I must decrease."

Romans 8:13-14 reminds us, "For if you live according to the flesh you will die; but if by the Spirit you put to death the deeds of the body, you will live. For as many as are led by the Spirit of God, these are sons of God."

He Put His Trust In The Name of the Lord
Another truth in the source of David's strength was that he put his trust in the Name of the Lord instead of swords, spears and shields. 2 Corinthians 10:4 says, "For the weapons of our warfare are not carnal, but mighty through God to the pulling down of strongholds." The weapons of our warfare are not carnal. Our weapons are not to manipulate the sense of reasoning and knowledge of ourselves or others. The weapons of our warfare are spiritual, and they are powerful. How did young David fight a lion with only a shepherd's rod? You take the Name of the Lord. The Name of the Lord is the all-powerful name. David learned not to trust in swords and spears. He learned that the weapons he needed to fight his battles were not the dagger of the eye, the sword of the tongue, or the shield made up of a group of people who agreed with his position. David learned that his strength lay in the fact that he trusted in the Name of the Lord.

We find an excellent illustration of David's trust in the Name of the Lord in 1 Samuel 17. In this chapter, we find David fighting the giant, Goliath. At the time of this confrontation, David was just a ruddy-faced lad. When Goliath saw David, he belittled him and said, "You come out here with a little shepherd's sling shot against me?!" That would be like taking a water pistol to a gun fight today. "You think I'm going to run off yapping like a dog because you hurl a stone in my direction? Why, I'm going to take you, you silly little runt, and I'm going to tear you into pieces and feed your flesh to the fowl of the air this very day!" David faced the giant (having already rejected the armor of Saul and the accompaniment of the rest of Saul's army because they had no faith) and he stood before Goliath and said (in vs.45-46), "You come to me with a sword, with a spear, and with a javelin. But I come to you in the name of the Lord of Hosts, the God of the armies of Israel, whom you have defied. This day the Lord will deliver you into my hand, and I will strike you and take your head from you. And this day I will give the carcasses of the camp of the Philistines to the birds of the air and the wild beasts of the earth, that all the earth may know that there is a God in Israel."

If you need miracles in your life, make up your mind to enter into faith in the name of God. Don't profane the name by failing to use it or by changing its meaning (that's taking the name of the Lord in vain.) Take the name of Jesus – take all the names of God – there is a name for every battle you face and every circumstance that arises. The name you take when the battle is finances is "Jehovah-jireh." The name you take when the battle is sickness is "Jehovah-rophe." The name you take when the battle is righteousness is "Jehovah-tsidkenu." Study every name of God, there is a weapon for every battle you will ever face in this life.

Praise and Worship
Praise and worship were significant truths as the source of David's strength. Most of the Psalms were written by David, a

chief musician, or by a prophet whom God appointed under David's ministry. David first wrote songs of praise when he was in the wilderness taking care of the sheep. All he had was his instrument and his shepherd's rod. David received the revelation of how great God is through praise and worship. I love to preach, I am called to preach, but I often receive more strength from the songs that we sing and lead during a worship service than I do from the preaching. Why? The Word, when set to music, engraves itself on the tables of our hearts. Scriptures that are set to music are much easier for me to remember. Sometimes I read a scripture during the week and get nothing out of it; then I come to church and start singing those words, and the fresh revelation comes – the word opens up and comes alive.

When we enter into praise and worship, the Word of God binds us to faith, joy, and a healthy expectation that we will run through the troops and leap over the walls. David spent many days and nights in praise and worship out in the field with the sheep. These times of fellowship were what prepared him to receive his call to his position as ministering king. David was used mightily by God, but we cannot expect God to do so with us if we neglect praise and worship. To neglect praise and worship will cause people to be argumentative, headstrong, rebellious and full of their own will, way, and ideas. It will cause people to either disregard the Holy Spirit or trample over Him. People who enter into praise and worship come under the anointing and sway of the Spirit. King Saul did not call for a psychiatrist, or for drugs or something to dull the brain when he was being tormented by demons; he had already tried all of those worldly remedies. Saul knew there was only one way to get relief. His relief came by calling for David and his harp. As David the minstrel entered Saul's oppressed filled tent, he entered into the king's court with praise and worship. The anointing of praise and worship will scatter and lift the weight of all oppressive and demonic spirits. When praise goes up, the devil goes down. When God's people enter into His gates with thanksgiving, and into His courts with praise, all oppression and demonic spirits go running out!

"Come before His presence with singing. Know that the Lord, He is God; It is He who has made us, and not we ourselves; we are His people and the sheep of His pasture. Enter into His gates with thanksgiving, and into His courts with praise. Be thankful to Him, and bless His name. For the Lord is good; His mercy is everlasting, and His truth endures to all Generations." (Psalm 100:3-5)

Praise and worship is the best medicine for anyone having problems with the demonic. When you are being troubled by the demonic, just start praising God. Don't immediately start looking for someone to cast out the demon or demand that it leave. Just enter into praise and worship. Praise and worship will drive the demons crazy and they will flee on their own. Demons have no place in our Christian life. I know some people are not going to agree with this next statement and may not continue reading on, however, the reality is that there are deliverance ministries that make the devil out to look frightening and powerful, but the devil has no power. Ministries that resort to that sort of thing are wasting their time. The devil cannot do more than God permits. I want that old serpent to know that I will no longer give him a platform or further opportunity, but I will praise and worship God instead. That is what will give us strength, power and might. When the Ark, (which symbolizes the presence of the Lord in the life of a believer) was being brought back to Jerusalem by David and his men, David could have ridden on a big horse in a processional, but he didn't. Instead, he took off his kingly garments and replaced them with the garments of a servant. As a servant, he acknowledged that the throne of Israel was the throne of God. He acknowledged that Jehovah, God Almighty, was the true King of Israel. The Ark of the Lord was brought back to Jerusalem, not by the Levitical priesthood (who had no way to go out and fight a battle for it) but by David, who was a praiser and worshipper. David was able to bring back the Ark because he entered into praise and worship. That was David's way of fighting the battle.

Psalm 57 and 59 give accounts of David praising the Lord when Saul tried to kill him. Instead of hiding and writing his last will and testament, David wrote Psalms about the victory and triumph of God. During those times when we seem to go from one calamity to another, we need to enter into praise and stay in it. We can choose to praise the Lord regardless of our circumstances. 1 Thessalonians 5:18 says, "In everything give thanks..." We do not praise the Lord to persuade Him to change the circumstances; we praise the Lord because praise binds us to Him. Our relationship is not to be based on houses, land, cars, how many people we have in our church service on Sunday morning, etc. Our concern should only be our relationship with Jesus Christ. David won another battle with praise and worship when his son, Absalom, came against him, ran him out of the city, and took his throne away from him. Nothing hurts more than your own family turning against you. That amount of pain can cause you to become so depressed and bereaved that you feel you have gone beyond the point of recovery as if you are going to die of a broken heart. But David conquered in these circumstances by getting into, and staying in, praise.

On one particular occasion, David came home, and his wife, Michal, scorned him, saying, "My husband made an absolute fool out of himself dancing before the damsels of Israel" (2 Sam.

6:16). David answered her ridiculing remarks by replying (paraphrased), "I have news for you, my dear wife, I am going to praise more tomorrow than I praised today." Many people attempted to discourage him from his times of praise, but he consistently said, "I will praise more." His insistence finally progressed to the point where he said he would praise five times a day, then seven times a day, then all day long. Then he said, "Let's have a choir, musicians, instruments and dancers. Let's praise through the night and through the day. Let the name of the Lord be praised twenty-four hours a day." David even praised when his baby died. In a time of death and bereavement, he stayed in praise. He said, "We fasted when the baby was sick. We mourned while he was in trouble. He cannot come back to us, but we can go to him. Wipe away your tears. Take off your sackcloth. Put on the garments of praise. Spread a feast, Praise the Lord." (2 Sam. 12:16-23)

It made no difference to David whether he was going through times of battle or times of leisure. He consistently praised the Lord. He praised when he was on the mountaintops. He praised when he was in the valleys. He praised the Lord in the mornings; he praised the Lord in the evenings. He praised the Lord on sunny days and on cloudy days. Psalm 34:1 sums up the depths of David's roar from his spirit with these unforgettable words of victory: "I will bless the Lord at all times: His praise shall continually be in my mouth." David's life was a continual demonstration of the power of anointed praise and worship.

Chapter 7
The Apostolic Anointing

The Five Truths of the Apostolic Anointing:

1. They were filled with the Holy Spirit.
2. They were filled with faith.
3. They were filled with grace. (Great grace was upon them.)
4. They had a prayer life. (If we are to enjoy the depth of the apostolic anointing, we will have to emulate the apostle's lives. As Paul said, he was often in prayer and fasting. Of the first apostles, Acts says they went to the temple to pray daily.)
5. They had a team ministry. They stood together (Acts 2). They prayed together. They gave witness together. They raised up the sick together. They went from house to house together, and they broke bread together.

"But as God is faithful, our word to you was not Yes and No. For the Son of God, Jesus Christ, who was preached among you by us—by me, Silvanus, and Timothy—was not Yes and No, but in Him was Yes. For all the promises of God in Him are yes, and in Him Amen, to the glory of God through us. Now He who establishes us with you in Christ and has anointed us is God, who also has sealed us and given us the Spirit in our hearts as a guarantee." (2 Cor. 1:18-22)

It is evident that this text is talking about the anointing and that its power wanes when there is a double mind; one time we say, "Yes, Lord," and another time we say, "No, Lord." We may say; "Yes, I'm not quitting! I'm going through, Jesus!" And another time we'll say, "I'm throwing in the towel! Let me out, Lord!" A person with a double mind is unstable in all his or her ways (James 1:8). In order to carry the kind of anointing the apostles carried, we must grow in Christ until we are able to stand in the same assurance of faith they did. They stood before their accusers (who had just beheaded one of their brothers and had stoned another, leaving him for dead), yet, they could say, "I know in whom I have believed, and death cannot separate me from the love of my God. I know Jesus is God manifest in the flesh. That's all there is to it and my testimony stands sure!"

So he said, "For the Son of God, Jesus Christ, who was preached among you by us, by me, Silvanus and Timothy, was not sometimes 'yes' and sometimes 'no', but when we preached him, it was always 'yes.'" That is, our gospel was always a positive gospel. Our gospel was always "God will do what He said He will do" (2 Cor. 1:18-22). God is not a man that He should lie and not the son of man that He should repent. The apostles had the kind of faith that says God is still in the business of doing what He said He would do. The days of miracles are not over. The days of revival are not over. The days of mighty power and demonstration of the Spirit are not over. When we affirm God's Word, we say, "Yes, Lord, You said it, I believe it. You have settled it and I stand on it!"

"God is not a man, that He should lie, nor a son of man, that He should repent. Has He said, and will He not do? Or has He spoken, and will He not make it good?" (Num. 23:19)

THE APOSTOLIC ANOINTING

2 Corinthians 1:20 KJV says, "For all the promises of God in Him are yes…" When we look to the church rather than Christ to fulfill the promises of God, the answers are sometimes "yes" and sometimes "no." For example, some preachers, especially if they are in a bad mood, have been known to say, "You can't have any of these blessings until you straighten up your act." But if we put the promises and blessings back onto Christ, they are always "yes" because He took all our sins and all our sorrows and the chastisement of our peace was upon Him (see Isa. 53). He does not come into our midst to punish us; He comes into our midst to deliver us.

Isaiah 53:4-5 states, "Surely He has borne our griefs and carried our sorrows; Yet we esteemed Him stricken, Smitten by God, and afflicted. But He was wounded for our transgressions, He was bruised for our iniquities; the chastisement for our peace was upon Him, and by His stripes we are healed."

Put the promises *in* Christ and get the Christ *in* you. Then you can always say, "Yes, it is true. This word in Him is true, and He is in me, and I am in Him, and His Word abides in me." To have the Word abiding in us does not mean to just have *memorized* scripture; it means to have *believed in* scripture. I practice *believing in* much more than I practice *memorizing* or *remembering* scripture. When I need it, because I believe in it, the Holy Spirit always brings it back to my memory. All the promises of God in Him are "yes," and in Him, "amen". The word *Amen* means "forevermore", "so let it be", or "so be it". *Amen* is more than a religious period at the end of a spiritual sentence. It is more than an agreement; it is a prophetic proclamation. Let it continue to be, world without end. Let no one find any excuse to say it will not continue to be so. All the promises of God are in Christ. Amen. If you are suffering with a disease, don't accept it as permanent or terminal. Get into the promises in Christ and say, "In Him they are 'yes' and 'amen'."

2 Corinthians 1:21 says, "Now He who establishes us with you in Christ and has anointed us is God." The Apostle Paul's message here is: God anointed Christ; God anointed the apostles with the same Christ-anointing; and that God is anointing all believers in both the Gentile and Jewish churches. But it had to be affirmed constantly, so that it was known by the Gentiles that the Jews had rights to the Messiah also. Paul deemed it essential for all to know that not only does the Messiah have an anointing from the Father, but the apostles have the same anointing from the Father, and now all the Gentiles of all nations, not just Jews, can be anointed and established together through Christ in God. What a tremendous truth!

We have no less anointing than the apostles had, and the apostles had no less anointing than Jesus had, and all the fullness dwelled in Him bodily. For this reason, Jesus said, "The works that I do shall you do also, because I go unto the Father" (John 14:12). He said, "And I will pray the Father, and He will give you another Helper, that He may abide with you forever—the Spirit of truth, whom the world cannot receive, because it neither sees Him nor knows Him; but you know Him, for He dwells with you and will be in you" (John 14:16-17). The Holy Spirit did not come upon the disciples as a dove in Acts 2 like he did with Jesus in Matthew 3:16; but rather He came upon them as flaming tongues of fire. The Holy Spirit could come upon Jesus as a dove because He had no sin. He was pure in spirit, pure in soul, pure in the flesh, and the dove could rest on Him. Since we have impure thoughts, attitudes, reactions, desires and emotions which need to be purged – we need the fire. However, the fire of God is not to be feared; it is our helper; it protects us from sin's domination in our life. We need the flow of the fire of the Spirit of God – that great and marvelous and wonderful anointing – continually.

The fire of God has two purposes:

1. It burns away what doesn't belong in us, but when it is done burning and purging out what doesn't belong in our lives.
2. It reveals our genuineness and the pure glory of God in us. We shine bright in Christ as pure gold. 1 Peter 1:7-8 says, "That the genuineness of your faith, being much more precious than gold that perishes, though it is tested by fire, may be found to praise, honor, and glory at the revelation of Jesus Christ, whom having not seen you love."

Again, 2 Corinthians 1:21 says, "Now He who establishes us with you in Christ and has anointed us is God..." God has anointed us; we don't anoint ourselves. When God anointed me and began showing me at age 16 up into my 20's that I was to preach the gospel, I was shocked! I thought God mixed me up with someone else. I thought for sure God had the wrong guy. Was there another Brian He had me confused with? I wanted to run in the opposite direction. I started to tell some people about what I was hearing and I am sure that they thought that I had lost my mind. I thought to myself, "God has better sense than to waste His anointing on a pitiful case such as mine." But, praise God, the anointing abides and it teaches us all things. Yes, it is God who calls and the one who chooses who He will anoint.

2 Corinthians 1:22 says, "Who also has sealed us and given us the Spirit in our hearts as a guarantee [as a deposit]." God

anointed us by giving us the Spirit, and the Holy Spirit is like a deposit in our hearts. We could say that a deposit is the first of many payments to come; or we could say a deposit is a filled vessel from which much more will be drawn. Both statements are correct. On the Day of Pentecost, the apostles were filled with the Holy Spirit. A few chapters later, we find them filled once more with the Holy Spirit. There is one baptism evidenced in speaking in other tongues (Mark 16:17; Acts 2:4-11; Acts 10:46; Acts 19:6; 1 Cor. 12:10-14.), but many fillings evidenced in a life of power and victory. To speak of the apostle's anointing is to speak of men who were constantly full of the spirit. There is a Bible pattern for filling up and staying filled with the Spirit. The general assembly of the local congregation is intended to be a place where prayer is so powerful that it fills you with the Spirit – a place where praises are so scripturally full of adoration to God and declaration of who He is that He inhabits our praises and we are filled with the Spirit.

In the last century, the work of the Spirit was to bring us into praise and worship. In the raising up of the Tabernacle of David, it was foretold (Acts 15:16), that the residue of men, the backslidden Edom, and the residue of unsaved Gentiles, would be drawn in. In every place where praise and worship has been in the last twenty years, it has drawn people into the house of God, but God will take us beyond the Tabernacle of David type renewal. In this next move, we will come into the apostle's anointing, where they went out into the streets, and door-to-door, and house-to-house, and into the temple daily. They got filled with the Spirit, and they stayed filled with the Spirit. They were filled with the Spirit so that they might become witnesses of Jesus Christ. The Bible says they went into all these areas – and lists different cities – and great multitudes of people were added unto the church until the news of it was heard in Jerusalem. Let us look at Acts 1:8 KJV, "But ye shall receive power, after that the Holy Spirit is come upon you: and ye shall be witnesses unto Me both in Jerusalem, and in all Judea, and in Samaria, and unto the uttermost part of the earth." This verse, in the original language, is very clear. It does not say, "You will be witnesses *for* me; it says you will be witnesses *unto* Me. There is a vast difference between witnessing for Jesus (telling people about Him) and witnessing unto Him (telling Him who you believe He is.)

One of our witnesses to Him is our prayer life. After the Holy Spirit comes upon us, we learn how to pray in the Spirit. Praying in the Spirit is different from praying with our understanding – which we are to do also. The Bible says in 1 Corinthians 14:2, "For he who speaks in a tongue does not speak to men but to God, for no one understands him; however, in the spirit he speaks mysteries." Romans 8:26-28 tells us that, "Likewise the Spirit also helps in our weaknesses. For we do not know what we should pray for as we ought, but the Spirit Himself makes intercession for us with groanings which cannot be uttered. Now He who searches the hearts knows what the mind of the Spirit is, because He makes intercession for the saints according to the will of God." The Holy Spirit prays through us, interceding for things we don't know how to pray for. Our own ability to pray – praying out of our own wants and knowledge might let us down, but when we begin to pray in the Spirit, our questions will be answered. He knows our future, our weaknesses, and our immediate situation. He starts praying through us for victory by the power of Jesus Christ.

Consider the reverse of witnessing unto God. It is possible to witness unto the devil. We witness unto the devil when we say, "There is a big, bad devil in my city. In fact, there are thousands of demons, and I believe they are focusing their attention on churches that are trying to move on with God." If we build up their name and their fame, we are witnessing unto the devil's kingdom and dominion. We witness unto Jesus by talking to Him; that is, "How great You are, Lord, You have cast down the enemy. You, Lord, have cast them into the sea!" We are anointed to be witnesses unto God not the devil. The Holy Spirit is not upon us for the purposes of being a witness to what our church or someone else's church will do. Neither is the Holy Spirit upon us to show the terrible trials that might be ahead. He anoints us to see the Christ who is the head, and the shield, to see the one who goes before and behind. The Holy Spirit anointing was not put upon us to forecast evil and darkness for the future, but to say unto the Christ, "You are my everything! Whether in my youth or my old age, you are the 'Great I Am.' You were the provider when I was sixteen years old as well as you will continue to be my provider when I am sixty years old. You are my everything!" He truly does get sweeter, richer, fuller and deeper as the days go by.

After you witness unto Him (after you know who you are, who He is, what He said, and what He can do) you have a "yes" confession to witness to the world. Then you can go into all Jerusalem, Judea, and Samaria and be a witness everywhere that Christ is raised from the dead. The primary message of the New Testament Church was: Jesus is risen and has ascended into heaven and has sent the Holy Spirit, another Comforter (just like Jesus), just as He promised, to move us to speak forth as His witnesses.

"But you shall receive power when the Holy Spirit has come upon you; and you shall be witnesses to Me in Jerusalem, and in all Judea and Samaria, and to the end of the earth." (Acts 1:8)

THE APOSTOLIC ANOINTING

The disciples were not thrown into jail for speaking in tongues. People understood the speaking in tongues. They didn't stand around on the day of Pentecost and say, "This is the devil, or this is weird religion." They said, "We hear these people glorifying God in our own language" (Acts 2:5-12). They were perplexed because they knew the apostles had not been through schooling to learn foreign languages. They said, "How could they be speaking in all these languages seeing they are just ignorant people from Galilee?" The answer was the Holy Spirit sent down from heaven came like a mighty wind on their soul, and they were bursting forth in languages, not learned by men, but in utterances given by a supernatural power. That supernatural power produced an anointing that exploded in the face of Jerusalem. In Acts 2:1-4; they all began to speak with tongues, and as they did, multitudes came and stood around until three thousand souls had been added to the church. All these souls were saved because Peter and the other apostles were full of the Holy Spirit and were anointed to preach the gospel of Jesus Christ. Christ should be the heart and center of all preaching and teaching. He is raised, alive with us; He is able, mighty and willing. He loves and He is touching humanity; still healing the sick, still opening blind eyes, still opening the ears of the deaf and still making the lame walk. He is not just the God of yesterday; He is also the God of today, and He is the God of all our tomorrows. All Praise be God! The world is not won by religious titles and hierarchy, but rather, we put on the Lord Jesus and wear the anointing like a robe, filled with the Holy Spirit and the anointing flows forth from us like a river.

The Lion's Anointing Is Full Of Faith
In Acts 3, five thousand souls were saved after the apostles happened upon and healed a lame man who had never walked.

ANOINTED TO ROAR

He asked the apostles (who were full of faith) for alms, but Peter said, "…silver and gold have I none; but such as I have give I thee: In the name of Jesus Christ of Nazareth rise up and walk" (Acts 3:6 KJV). He took the crippled man by the right hand and lifted him up, and immediately the man's anklebones received healing and strength. He leaped up, stood for a while, and then walked without their assistance. The only assistance he had was the anointing.

Peter and John were full of faith. They roared out from the depths of their spirit and told the man to look on them; not for gold or silver, nor for psychology and human wisdom, but for what they had in the Spirit. What did they have? They had the Lion's anointing! They had this anointing because they were full of the Holy Spirit and full of faith. Peter told those who witnessed the miracle, "It was not our own power or holiness that made this man walk; it was through faith in the name of Jesus." At this point you might say, "When am I going to get that full and have that kind of roar?" You will get that full when you increase your prayer life. The more you spend time with the Lion of Judah, the more you will be like, look like, act like and roar like the Lion of Judah.

The apostles were on their way to prayer. They went to prayer at the ninth hour every day. It is important to establish a daily prayer life, and when you pray, do not just seek the Lord for help to survive another day, but seek Him to be full of the Spirit. Instead of saying, "Oh God, just keep me going for another day." We need to focus a little higher and say, "Lord, fill me with the Holy Spirit until the Lion's anointing flows out of me, and I meet someone at the gate beautiful and am anointed to roar over them, 'such as I have, and I know I have it because I am overflowing in it.'" When you don't know you have the anointing, it most likely is not flowing. When it is overflowing, you know you have it. Sometimes, when I minister in prayer lines, I sense that I am half emptied out. So I will stop and say, "Let's worship. Let's sing until we get full of the Spirit," and then the anointing starts flowing again. When you are full enough, it will overflow, and the overflow does the ministering. The more I am in the Lion's presence, the more I realize how spiritually needy I am. It takes a lot to satisfy my spiritual hunger. I have always been like that from the moment I was saved. Spiritual neediness means I am conscious that there is nothing in me that can please God. There is nothing in me that can meet the divine standard. There is nothing in me, out of human effort, which can qualify me for the race. I need the touch of God in everything I do. I need the anointing the apostles had that caused them to walk in and out among their persecutors, stand in the face of all their threats and say, "We can't help, but to declare the things we have seen and heard. We are eye witnesses of His majesty and glory. We have heard the Lion roar and do tremble in His presence."

The apostles preached with great power because they saw Jesus go up in the cloud. They saw the angels come out of the cloud. They heard Him say, "Go and tarry in Jerusalem until you be endued with power" (see Luke 24:49). The apostolic anointing of power was so great that it is said, "In a few years, these men have turned the world upside down." The Bible reveals that in the apostolic era, great multitudes were brought and laid in the streets, and they were all healed. The anointing was so powerful that when the shadow of Peter fell across them, they were healed, revived, restored and went back to their villages and they were made whole. The apostle's roar was full of faith and power. They said, "What we have, we give to you." What they had was the Lion within them that when they roared out in His likeness, strength, and name that it made every sickness, disease, and demon in hell scatter! In Acts 3, the people wondered, "How is this done? What is this all about?" Peter answered, "The name of Jesus has made this man whole." They put the name of Jesus right out there in front. Today, many Christians are putting every other kind of name out in front. They use all kinds of names to describe the conditions in which people are imprisoned, but the apostles didn't list any of those things. When they brought a man out of prison, they said, "It's the name of Jesus that has freed you!"

I may run the risk of sounding like an old time preacher here, but I feel the lion's roar bubbling up on the inside of me and I have to tell it like it really is. We need to get back to an old-fashioned, Holy Spirit led, praising and praying, genuine church again. The days of the apostolic miracle flow (as described in the book of Acts) will come again! We will see people delivered by the power of God, through faith in His name. As we roar the name of Jesus, with a lion's anointing, people will jump, the crippled will leap, and the anointing will flow. The crippled will be lined up fifty deep in their wheelchairs and someone will tell them, "Roar out and say, 'Jesus'!" They will all roar together and say "Jesus!", and half of them will jump out of their wheelchairs and run all over the place. Then someone will say to the other half (those who are still crippled), "Roar out the name of Jesus once more." They will say "Jesus!" one more time. Then, they will also jump out of their wheelchairs and run with the others. The name of Jesus contains power, anointing and faith that will release the overflow.

For many, the name of Jesus has become just lines of a song, or part of a ritual or ceremony. People want ceremonies because they have put the name of Jesus into an ancient, stagnant, lifeless ceremonial role, but there is power in the name of Jesus! The name of Jesus is the name in which every knee shall bow. It is the name in which every demon spirit is silenced. It is the name in which every sin evaporates. It is the name in which every bent and twisted body is released and straightened. It is by His name that we are filled with faith. We should all continue to study the names of the Lord; for the name of the Lord is like a bottle of healing ointment poured out upon the soul. The Lord recently spoke to me about more anointing. He said, "I am going to give you a more powerful anointing and open up to you things out of the Book that you have not yet understood. I will give My people the kind of things I gave to other men and women in other times – things that released and brought about miracles. These promises are still in the Book, and I am going to reveal them, and you will see them. Yes, and when you see them you will declare them -- roar them out over the nations!"

In recent times, the devil has been telling Christians to 'retire.' He's telling them to retire from church, prayer, witnessing, preaching and prophesying. *Retire* is just another word for quitting. The Father in heaven is fanning His holy flame, and it is sweeping through the church again. The fire is burning again; it can be seen in the faces of many. However, there are others who are still peering through the bars with a gaunt look wondering if God has passed them by. One of these days, the earth will shake at the roar of the King of Kings, Jesus, and the prisoners will come out as they did at Philippi.

"And when they had laid many stripes on them, they threw them into prison, commanding the jailer to keep them securely. Having received such a charge, he put them into the inner prison and fastened their feet in the stocks. But at midnight Paul and Silas were praying and singing hymns to God, and the prisoners were listening to them. Suddenly there was a great earthquake, so that the foundations of the prison were shaken; and immediately all the doors were opened and everyone's chains were loosed. And the keeper of the prison, awaking from sleep and seeing the prison doors open, supposing the prisoners had fled, drew his sword and was about to kill himself. But Paul called with a loud voice, saying, "Do yourself no harm, for we are all here." Then he called for a light, ran in, and fell down trembling before Paul and Silas. And he brought them out and said, "Sirs, what must I do to be saved?" (Acts 16:23-30)

Finally, in Acts 4, we read the rest of the story concerning the healing of the crippled man. It says that the multitudes that believed were of one heart (in unity) and with great power the apostles witnessed (inner roar) to the resurrection of Jesus Christ. When we start preaching more on the resurrection of Christ, drug addicts will stop taking drugs. They will receive the revelation of the resurrected Christ. They may just take the free Bible you put in their hand and walk away starry-eyed and swaying still under the influence of their drugs. But many will come back later and say, "That Bible you gave me opened my eyes and Jesus delivered me from a life of drug addiction." We are coming to a day when with great power we will again give witness unto the message of the resurrection of Jesus Christ. Being full of faith will cause you to look for the good in everything. It will cause you to look at a crippled person and say, "This is not punishment, this is for the glory of God." Some people who are not full of faith say that being crippled or sick is "punishment for your many sins." Or they say, "This is the devil," or "This is a curse from God." But those who are full of faith will say, "This is God's opportunity to show you His grace and His power!" It is not God putting a chain around someone's neck; it is God offering someone the key to a miracle. You may not have the key at the moment; you may just have the door the key goes in, but someone, somewhere, has the key to your miracle.

Great Grace Was Upon Them

When you are full of the Holy Spirit and faith, you sense the favor of God. You think about God in loving terms. You think about Jesus as your best friend. You think about church in favorable terms. When the grace of God comes upon you, you want to be in worship and prayer and in church services. When the leader says, "It is time to quit praising," you say, "Oh, no, I want to praise longer; can't we do just one more song?" When grace comes upon you, you feel the favor of God; you feel like you belong. You feel important. You feel energized. You feel like you can do all things through Christ who gives you strength (see Phil. 4:13).

During my early elementary school years, I never felt like I belonged. I never felt like I quite fit in with the rest of the kids. I had a box haircut and had to wear big black thick coke bottle type eye glasses (thanks Mom!), and as many of you already know from your own experiences in school, kids will be kids and so I found myself (and my nerdy looks), in the punch line of many jokes and much teasing. In today's culture, they would call that *bullying*. As a result of all the teasing, I had a very poor self-image so I never felt important. It bothered me so much that I absolutely dreaded having to go to school every day to face such rejection. It was not until the 6th grade that I felt the need to take matters into my own hands and change my deplorable course. I began telling myself that I was going to make every necessary change to my looks and personality to gain the acceptance and favor I was so desperately looking for among my peers. I was determined that I would no longer be laughed at or be pushed around. So I began the journey of my extreme makeover to

105

change my looks and my desperate condition. I made my mother take me down to the mall and buy me new clothes and shoes that were "in style". I begged her to take me to the hairdresser to change my hairstyle. I asked her if she would buy me some new "cool glasses" to go with my new look. She graciously did all the above and I must say that it was a huge improvement from what I used to look like. People began to take notice of me. I thought it was pretty funny that one kid whom I had shared a few classes with for a year thought I was a new student who had just transferred into the school from another state. The most memorable improvement for me was to see the pretty girls come out from the shadows of the school breezeways and taking notice that I was alive! I also waited for the very next popular bully to try and make me the center of his lunchtime comedy routine. I walked right up to him and punched him square in the nose! Of course, it had to be one of the bigger bullies in the school yard so it took more than one punch to take that mean giant down, but nevertheless, I earned every other school bullies respect that day. Yet, in spite of all that I had done to improve myself and gain the popularity, approval, and favor of the people at my school I still felt rejected and at times of little value. Instead of my life taking a dramatic turn for the better, it took a drastic turn for the worse as I was always trying to prove my value and worth; to "prove something" to the world. This led me into much trouble, sin, and rebellion, but in the latter part of my high school years, I was saved and filled with the Holy Spirit. Great grace came upon me and I felt the favor of God come upon my life, and I no longer felt the scorn of men. I felt the acceptance of God and not the rejection of and the comparison of others my age. When they cussed, I would not. When they would party, I would run to church. When they would get mad and call me a "holy roller," I wouldn't take my revenge and beat them up. I would say, "I would rather be a fool for Jesus than a fool for the world and the devil." I began to have favor with all the students and the teachers. I had so much grace upon me that I knew I would go to heaven if I died, but if my friends died in their sins, they would go to hell. I knew I understood more than they did. I knew I ought to tell them of God's love, and because I had great grace upon my soul, I told them what I knew. Many of my friends and family members gave their lives to Jesus Christ; not because of my influence in their lives, but because of His influence and favor they saw resting upon me. Jesus had made the change in me; He did in me what I could never do for myself.

I now come to the pulpit week after week and roar like a lion when I preach. It's not because I am a professional preacher – but because of the anointing of the Holy Spirit. When the anointing comes upon you and you become full of the Holy Spirit and full of faith, you talk like you believe what you are talking about. You talk like you know what you are talking about. You talk like you know who is behind what you say. You walk in the midst of the grassy fields of your life like a strong, wise, cunning, anointed king of the beasts! Many times, while speaking, I come to the end of my knowledge. It's then, by the anointing, words beyond my wisdom begin to kick in and continue to come forth, and people say, "Pastor that wasn't just you talking to us today, it was God!"

The apostles had so much grace upon their lives that they were able to walk through and endure all the persecution and rejection of their day. In their day, if you left Judaism and accepted Christ, your family disowned you. They would have had a burial for you and would have mourned for you. The first century believers suffered extreme persecution and rejection, yet they continued to preach Christ and to proclaim that Christianity would fill the earth. This witness will go to every nation, tribe, language and generation. People will preach the gospel with the Holy Spirit and power sent down from heaven. These people will be so full of faith that they will prophetically roar over the crippled, "Rise!" and say to the blind, "Your eyes are being opened!"

The apostolic anointing is not reserved for special people in the hierarchies of ecclesiastical settings. These anointings to roar flows in this fashion:

1. These signs shall follow them that believe.
2. In My Name, they shall cast out devils.
3. They shall heal the sick.
4. They shall drink deadly things and they will not be hurt.
5. They shall lay hands on the sick and the sick shall recover.

The full apostolic anointing has been bottled up in a little vessel, with a cork, wick, and a light, through a lack of respect for God's chosen order and Holy Spirit government. Sometimes you think "Wow, my Pastor must be an Apostle." Other times you think "Wow, my Pastor is a jerk." Sometimes you think "This man must be a true prophet", and other times you think "This man is off his rocker." But in spite of all his positive and negative feedback his little light continues to flicker, so he must be for real. It is time for the plug to come out and the little burning flax to be put away. It is time for the oil to overflow until every man, woman, boy and girl in the Kingdom says, "I have what the Apostle Paul had... I have the anointing to roar with the Lion of the tribe of Judah!" Or "I have the anointing that Peter had... I have the Lion's authority and anointing that roars into the deepest demonic pit and declares, "...you are Peter, and on this rock I will build My church, and the gates of Hades shall not prevail against you! (See Matt. 16:18)

God has anointed me with Jesus Christ, the Lion's anointing. I am not just a follower; I am a fellow heir of God and of Jesus Christ. I am anointed to roar! I am the son of the Lion and the successor of the pride of lions, and the works that He did, I am now doing. I am not going to sit down and say, I want a comfortable seat in the pew (comfortable grassy plain). I am not going to go on the charismatic carousel all over town, from church to church, to find the perfect church (not going from one pride to another flaunting my roar). I am going into the prayer closet daily to seek God, and I will stay there until I can come out and not say that I go to this particular church or I am under that particular Pastor, but that Jesus is risen and He is the Head of the whole Church throughout all the earth." Jesus is the Lion King and has all authority, power, might, and dominion!

Even to this day, the Lord is showing how to release the mighty roar (the power of the Holy Spirit) of which who's sound is wrapped up in the Name of Jesus. Sometimes He shows us how to roar in meetings, in the local church. At other times, He shows us how to roar through the moving of the Spirit through International TV ministries. Then, on other occasions, He shows us how to roar through the writing of books, and other times His roaring is done by door-to-door evangelism. Through many means and methodologies His roar shall be heard in all the earth and this gospel of the kingdom will be preached (roared out) in all the world as a witness to all the nations. (See Matt. 24:14)

Chapter 8
The Prayer Anointing

Posture of Prayer

In order for a lion to roar effectively, he must first adjust his posture. The unleashing of such a roar requires a bow. His head drops, and he expands his chest to fill his lungs with air. If we are ever to produce a roar of such magnitude, it will require a change in our present posture. To roar operatively, we must drop our high-held heads and bow down. This is a stance of humility and prayer will position us to receive a fresh infilling of the breath of God's Spirit.

"Therefore prophesy against them all these words, and say to them: 'The Lord will roar from on high, and utter His voice from His holy habitation; He will roar mightily against His fold. He will give a shout, as those who tread the grapes, against all the inhabitants of the earth.'" (Jer. 25:30)

Anointed Prayer

By *anointed prayer*, we mean any prayer that gives a place to the Holy Spirit. An anointed prayer can be prayed in tongues or a common, understood language. Your prayers will be anointed when you recognize the need, presence and work of the Holy Spirit. The anointing can come one drop at a time, and at other times, it comes pouring out like water from a faucet. Then, at other times it is rubbed in like a medicated ointment. No matter what form the Holy Spirit comes in, if it is mixed with faith we will enjoy all the benefits of its intended manifestation.

Matthew 13:53-54 says, "Now it came to pass, when Jesus had finished these parables, that He departed from there. When He had come to His own country, He taught them in their synagogue, so that they were astonished and said, 'Where did this Man get this wisdom and these mighty works?' The answer, of course, is: He received them while on His knees in prayer. Anointed prayer is the basis and beginning of a victorious life. Without anointed prayer, nothing will reach its full potential, regardless of what we do, what skills we have, or what talents and abilities we have been given. God works on the principle of line upon line, precept upon precept, here a little and there a little (see Isa. 28:13). We tend to pray a while and then get busy doing things, then later come back to praying over the same thing. One problem we have with prayer is that we want to be like bulldozers and just rev up, put down the blade, and bulldoze everything out of the way in about ten minutes. We want to shake the dust off ourselves and say, "I've prayed, and now I've got the victory." Remember the principle is, *a little here, a little there, line upon line*; it is he who keeps knocking, he who keeps asking, that will get the answers. You say, "Pastor, I have already asked a hundred times!" Well, there is a man who can relate to you in the Bible. Apparently this man asked every day for thirty-eight years as he was brought to the temple and laid at the gate Beautiful (see Acts 3:2-10). He was looking for help, and he was looking for mercy. After thirty-eight long years, he was still asking. He built a faith that was irresistible. He never became weary in well doing – and finally, the power of the Spirit moved and he received his answer! Galatians 6:9 KJV says, "And let us not be weary in well doing; for in due season we shall reap, if we faint not." If you keep praying, you shall receive the reward of anointed prayer. Prayer always reaps the greatest reward. How often should we pray? Is there a scripture that tells us how often we should pray? Should we pray three times a day, or ten times a day? Philippians 4:6 says, "Be anxious for nothing, but in everything by prayer and supplication, with thanksgiving, let your requests be made known to God..." Notice the emphasis is on "in everything". This is saying that we should, at all times and in everything we do, be praying and interceding with an attitude of thanksgiving. So instead of grumbling when we do the dishes we should pray, "Thank you Jesus for the food we have enjoyed that got these plates so messy in the first place." When we have to mow the lawn, instead of saying, "Why do I have to be out here in this blazing one hundred and fifteen degree Arizona temperature? That's it! I'm done! I am moving to the cool country of Colorado..." We should pray and ask God to make us content in the city where we live because it's where He placed us. We ask God to minister to us where we are until "He decides" to put us somewhere else. We pray in everything; at all times and in all places. In everything, by anointed prayer and supplication and thanksgiving, we let our requests be made known to God. There are many ways to pray, but in this lesson, we are going to explore the heights and depths, and the ins and outs, of anointed prayer.

Pray With Music

This is one way of praying that some people have not thought of in the church for centuries. I didn't accidentally stumble onto this truth; it was my spiritual father who did many years ago. I was blessed enough to be shown by him how to pray along with music and to see it demonstrated in a very practical, yet powerful way in the cutting-edge, spiritually advanced, prophetic church that I grew up in called Sweetwater Church of the Valley. My Pastor was under the notion, most of his Christian life, that music could be either a distraction and tool of the devil to invoke sin and pleasures of the flesh, or it could be used for mere entertainment. In his early years, he thought that all prayer was more or less a religious punishment. To be honest, I had similar feelings about prayer growing up in the Catholic Church, except that my perceptions were one that said a person only prayed to make some sort of penitence for something they or someone else did wrong. Sometimes, when prayer is the subject of a special teaching or sermon, people's minds go back to unpleasant experiences they had at the family altar when they were children. They were forced to come into the house to pray, and then Mom and Dad argued over who was going to pray. The kids would cry, and Mom and Dad would end up fighting. People who have had experiences like this do not want this type of a family altar in their homes. They don't see prayer as an exciting, positive experience. Then there are others which have had some other disappointing experiences in prayer, such as praying hard and fast, and surrendering it all to God for someone who was either sick or dying and then the person they prayed for died. Some of these negative memories associated with prayer can be displaced when there is music playing in the background while you are praying. Music lifts the spirit; it does something to your heart. It is very beneficial to have worship music and gospel recordings playing in your car, your home, and in your prayer room. Sometimes when you are praying with music, there are words along with the music, and those words come alive in your mind, agree in your spirit, and your faith rises to the level of the prophetic words of the music.

One time, while in Bible college, I was on a flight coming home to visit my family for the holidays. The turbulence on that flight became so bad that I could not muster up the faith to say, "Peace, be still," to the storm I was facing. The only thing I could think to do was take out my Walkman CD player and headphones, play a worship CD, close my eyes, and begin to pray along with the worship music that reminded me what God promised concerning my destiny. I was going to travel the world preaching the gospel of Jesus Christ. I reminded Him that I hadn't done any of those things prophesied just yet, and I didn't think that would look so good for Him if He decided to take me to heaven in a plane crash just traveling across the states from Dallas, Texas to Phoenix, Arizona. That was hardly "across the world!" Once the music started playing, faith began to rise up within me. The music helped bring me to peace so that I could pray in faith, and stay calm and be assured for the remainder of the flight.

Have you ever become so tortured with loneliness that you come under tremendous assault of demonic powers? When it is two o'clock in the morning and you feel lonely and sense demonic oppression, it is extremely difficult to muster up an "In the name of Jesus!" There are times in these depths of loneliness that you cannot even speak a word, but you can learn what worship music can do to aid you in anointed prayer. In these times and seasons I encourage you to put a good Spirit-filled worship recording in one of your electronic listening devices and fill the room with worship music. As your spirit begins to lift, start praising and rejoicing. I guarantee that the demons of loneliness will start fleeing. The Holy Spirit enters, and your loneliness will be gone and you will go back to feeling comforted, loved, and not alone. If you need to, go to sleep to the sound of sweet worship music, and wake up the next morning to a day free of loneliness and demonic oppression. The help you need comes through anointed prayer accompanied by wonderful Spirit-filled worshipful music.

Pray With The Scriptures

Prayer does not have to be original. In times past, churches used prayer books. These prayer books contained prayers based upon and including portions of the Scriptures, to aid people in prayer. Jesus prayed the Scripture in the wilderness. When the devil tempted Him to work a miracle to prove who He was, Jesus replied, "It is written…" When you find yourself going through a trial, the best thing to do is to go through the Bible and find ten to twenty Scriptures that speak to your particular situation. Then, every time you pray about that situation, pray those Scriptures. They add a dimension that could never be added by your own thoughts and imaginations. I have discovered that the most edifying form of praying the Scriptures is to pray Bible prayers or the Psalms. So often prayers found in the Bible, like the Lord's Prayer, or Daniel's prayer (see Matt. 6:9-13 & Dan. 9:1-27), touch so deeply that they release our faith more than our own words might. Audibly praying most of the Psalms releases faith, hope and joy. There is a psalm for every mood (good, bad, or ugly) and every need. Pray the Psalms, the Word of God – which is quick and powerful and discerns the thoughts and intents of our heart and reveals the hidden thoughts of our soul (see Heb. 4:12). When the soul is exposed to the revelation of the Word, the anointing is immediately applied to the wound or the festering sore. God not only answers prayer, but also heals and changes us from glory to glory.

Pray With Joy and With Sorrow

Every now and then, someone approaches me saying, "I've lost my prayer ministry." I explain to them that it is impossible for them to lose their prayer ministry. Losing your prayer ministry is like losing Jesus or the Holy Spirit, and it is impossible to lose them, especially when Jesus said Himself, "And lo, I am with you always, even to the end of the age" (Matt. 28:20). God's Word says that His anointing abides in us always, even if you feel dry and abandoned in the wilderness, He will never abandon you. I have also experienced this feeling of losing my prayer ministry, I understand what others are experiencing. Generally, what they are experiencing is a loss of joy and excitement. They have lost the bubbling joy of prayer, but it is not necessary for us to have bubbling joy in order to pray. We can pray with sorrow. Sorrow can drive you to your knees where you pour out your soul to the Lord in ways that you never could previously. This can bring you some of the greatest answers, the greatest insights, and the greatest growths you could ever experience. In 1 Samuel 1, Hannah poured out her bitterness before the Lord. Afterwards, she received not only comfort, but also her answer. It came in the birth of the son she so desperately prayed for and desired. Sometimes our prayers of sorrow are the avenues to the joy we think we have lost.

Pray With Tongues

Have you ever been praying when someone else in your congregation that always prays in tongues becomes a distraction, and you wonder why they always have to pray in tongues? I have had that happen to me often growing up in a prophetic, Spirit-filled church. I have had experiences in my anointed prayer life where other peoples' praying in tongues disturbed me, and I thought that if they could have only changed languages, or if they would have just lowered their volume, it would have been okay. However, now I have learned that what you must do in this situation is bring your mind back onto what you are doing, and on your conversation with God. Just get shut in with God. When you do, you will realize that others' styles of prayer will not conflict with yours. Praying in tongues is one of the greater gifts that God has bestowed upon the human race. Praying in tongues has been one the greatest gifts that God has ever bestowed upon my life personally. Praying in tongues makes it possible for you to pray to God in secret... So much in secret that not even the devil knows what you are saying. If there is a reason for the tongues spoken to be understood, the Holy Spirit supplies the gift of interpretation. Praying in tongues is never praying to other people. The scripture says in 1 Corinthians 14 that he who prays in an unknown tongue prays to God, not to man.

There are three kinds of tongues:

1. The evidence that you have been baptized with the Holy Spirit.
2. The Spirit praying in you, making intercession for you, praying for things you do not know how to pray for on your own (the mysteries of heaven).
3. A loving expression of admiration of God, for who He is to us as individuals, not for what He does for us.

Pray With Understanding

Those who are naturally poetic can create a prayer that sounds magnificent, but few of us are natural poets. Most of us have a problem speaking fluently to our own fathers, and even more so to our Heavenly Father. When I pray, I frequently hear myself using adjectives where adverbs should be used, or getting my objects in the wrong place, or getting the tenses wrong. One of my worst subjects in school growing up was English and Grammar. This is why I don't easily recognize my mistakes now. All I can say is thank God for skilled book editors or this book would be an utter disaster of adjectives, nouns, adverbs, conjunctions, and objects all imploding together! But, thank God, He has shown me that even though I do not have perfect grammar, I can still pray with understanding. Even if our words are backward, upside down, and mixed up, God knows what we mean. We can even pray the wrong prayer and get the right answer. He knows what we have need of even before we ask. (See Matt. 6:8)

Pray With Praise

It is good to pray with praise. It is also good to pray until praise rises spontaneously. Some of us would call that "praying through." Years ago, some Christians lived in almost constant depression because they thought that believers should be victorious 24 hours a day, 7 days a week. They thought victory should be evidenced by excitement, enthusiasm, joy, and the absence of trials. If they had trials, they lost their joy, and if they lost their joy, they lost their enthusiasm. Upon that basis, they wondered if they had lost their Christianity, and so they became depressed. They would start out their prayers in a state of depression. They would pray from one level to another level until a little bit of praise would begin to flow. Then when the praise would continue to flow out like a river, they began to "feel like" they had the victory. Then, once they felt like they had the victory, they would quit praying and proclaim that they had the victory. This is not the best example on how to pray with praise. We are learning to pray with praise at all times and in all places; not praise that is from joy only, but praise that is from the choice of faith. Now we choose to praise God because we know He wants us to praise Him. In fact, He dwells in our praises. The obedience to faith that Paul speaks of in Romans 16 and in Hebrews 11 is possible for each of us, as we develop the kind of faith that the book of Romans teaches. He says that God blesses those who seek His face with all the blessings of the everlasting covenant.

"But without faith it is impossible to please Him, for he who comes to God must believe that He is, and that He is a rewarder of those who diligently seek Him." (Heb. 11:6)

119

Pray With Pain

Sometimes when we pray with pain, the sounds we make sound like we should be in a hospital emergency room. Before the great revivals broke out, and before mankind learned how to walk in the evangelical joy and faith that we know today, the church believed in suffering instead of rejoicing. In some parts of the world today, many churches are still under pre-revival eras, like they were in the dark ages. They believe the more you suffer, the holier you will be; while we post-revivalists believe the more joyful we become, the greater is our expression of victory. They believe sadness is an expression of consecration and dedication; that the more you cry at the altar, the more spiritual you are. When people are praying in their pain, it is difficult to get into a frame of mind where they can praise the Lord. No one should disqualify themselves because they are praying out of a place of pain; God still hears their prayers. Pain is sometimes a result of our level of growth. Can you remember being ten years old and wishing you were fourteen? Or being fourteen and wishing you were eighteen? Or being fifty and wishing you were twenty? Regardless of the pain that grips you, prayer will build you up. Anointed prayer will make life's circumstances less painful and turn the pain into gain. Anointed prayer will turn your numbing deep emotional soar into a Spirit-filled joyful roar!

Pray With Hope

Many people are bound by hopelessness, thinking it disqualifies them from prayer. When you are hopeless is when you need to pray the most. We can pray when we are full of hope, but we can also pray when we feel hopeless. I have been in prayer when I could see no reason for hope. God would then begin to reveal little things to my heart, which would make me rise to my feet and say, "I hope again because God is God; He is the same yesterday, today, and forever! Through the good, the bad, and ugly of life He remains the same – He is always good!"

Anointed Prayer With Faith

There are times when the Spirit prays through us with faith, which enables us to pray in spite of doubt. Faith and doubt can exist in the same mind about the same subject, and we can be torn between the two. Jesus even said in Matthew 17:21, "However, this kind does not go out except by prayer and fasting." It isn't that we don't have faith, but that we have doubt encumbering our faith with questions. The purpose of fasting and anointed prayer is not to gain more power with God, but to resolve the question that arises because of doubt. When these questions are resolved, we can speak in faith with no doubt. So, when you have doubts, don't quit praying; pray more. Through anointed prayer, your doubts will disappear.

"….he who doubts is like a wave of the sea driven and tossed by the wind. For let not that man suppose that he will receive anything from the Lord; he is a double-minded man, unstable in all his ways." (James 1:6-8)

"So Jesus answered and said to them, 'Have faith in God. For assuredly, I say to you, whoever says to this mountain, be removed and be cast into the sea, and does not doubt in his heart, but believes that those things he says will be done, he will have whatever he says. Therefore I say to you, whatever things you ask when you pray, believe that you receive them, and you will have them.'" (Mark 11:22-24)

Pray In Silence Or Out Loud

There are three ways we can pray:

ANOINTED TO ROAR

1. We can pray in silence.
2. We can pray in groanings.
3. We can pray with great volume.

The first, praying in silence, is mostly neglected by Evangelical Charismatic Pentecostal type churches. When my spiritual father first came into the Charismatic Renewal in the late 1960's, he and his church were full blown Pentecostals. I remember him telling me a story how ten Pentecostals could make more noise than a thousand Charismatics. His church started moving and growing in the Charismatic flow. One day, he was leading his church in a prayer meeting and the building was packed, but it was so quiet you could almost have heard a pin drop. He thought to himself, "These people don't know how to pray." Then he started praying louder and louder; he felt as if he was trying to pump air into a flat tire. Then the Holy Spirit spoke to him and said, "What are you doing?" He said, "I'm trying to get these people to pray." The Holy Spirit said, "Your problem is that your idea of prayer is a greater volume; My idea of prayer is having the right attitude. You do not understand that people can pray in silence with the right attitude and get the answers they need, while you pray with a lot of noise and with the wrong attitude – judging others – and get no answers." So, he and his congregation quickly learned to pray in silence. There are times when praying out loud could get you into trouble, for instance in a court of law. If you prayed out loud there, you would get charged with contempt of court. You can silently whisper a prayer to God in a courtroom or any environment and the Holy Spirit will quiet your heart and soul and bring your answers just as quickly as when you were loudly and boldly praying down the house in a church-wide prayer meeting.

THE PRAYER ANOINTING

Pray Alone Or Pray In Crowds

In the early years of my 33 year long journey of learning to walk with God and prayer, for years I felt as if I had to be alone to feel I had touched God. Later in my ministry, I went in the opposite direction in relation to my praying. I became accustomed to praying in crowds, and I got out of balance. I did not feel that God was with me unless there was a large group of special anointed people around me. We need to learn to build an anointed prayer life in every environment we find ourselves in; whether in our public life or our private life. There are seasons where we need to be in our personal prayer closet alone, and shut in with God, and then there are seasons where we need to be in a group standing in united fervent corporate prayer. Here are two examples of both personal and public prayer (although there are many more examples in scripture to compare than just these two listed).

The first example is found in Matthew 6 where Jesus after a short discourse on the follies of trying to appear religious in front of people, Jesus talks about prayer. "And when thou prayest, thou shalt not be as the hypocrites are: for they love to pray standing in the synagogues and in the corners of the streets, that they may be seen of men. Verily I say unto you, they have their reward. But thou, when thou prayest, enter into thy closet, and when thou hast shut thy door, pray to thy Father which is in secret; and thy Father which seeth in secret shall reward thee openly. But when ye pray, use not vain repetitions, as the heathen do: for they think that they shall be heard for their much speaking. Be not ye therefore like unto them: for your Father knoweth what things ye have need of, before ye ask him" (Matt. 6:5-8 KJV). The Greek word used here for *"closet"* is *tameion* which means "an inner storage chamber or a secret room." The point being, a public prayer, announced on a street corner, gives the pray-er all the attention he can expect to receive. A quiet prayer, directed at God and not passers-by, will reap spiritual blessings.

Some have taken the admonition literally. They set aside a room or a quiet corner in their homes, furnish it with a comfortable chair, table, Bible, and maybe a notebook or journal, and use that corner for a regular prayer time. That's certainly appropriate, but the room Jesus referred to most likely meant "a pantry." A prayer closet might be a daily commute, a bench in the back yard, or the kitchen table. John Wesley's mother is said to have sat in a chair and thrown her apron over her head as a sign to her kids to leave her alone. Jesus usually went to a secluded hillside. The point is that the closet is free from interruption, distraction, and listening ears. Although there are good reasons to have a dedicated space for regular prayer—such as training the family to respect the quiet, and keeping prayer-related materials in one place—that was not what Jesus was referring to. The passage in Matthew 6 talks about performing religious acts for the purpose of allowing others to see. Any act, be it praying, giving, or serving, should not be done for the purpose of gaining approval from others. Praying, giving, and serving should be responses to our relationship with God and the mercies He has given us. If a specific, dedicated location encourages prayer, it should by all means be used. If the cab of a pickup or a quiet stretch of beach suffices, that's perfectly acceptable.

The second example is that of public prayer. Many Christians struggle with the idea of praying in public. Since many believers were known to pray in public in the Bible, as did Jesus Himself, there is nothing wrong with public prayer. Many O.T. leaders prayed publicly for the nation. Solomon prayed in front of the entire nation for them and himself. There is nothing to indicate that this prayer was not acceptable to the Lord (see 1 Kings

8:22-23). After the return of the Israelites from the Babylonian captivity, Ezra was so overwhelmed by the knowledge that the Israelites had left the worship of the true God that he prayed and wept bitterly before the house of the Lord. So fervent was his prayer that it prompted, "A very large assembly of men, women, and children," to gather with him and weep bitterly (see Ezra 10:1). However, the examples of Hannah and Daniel illustrate that it is possible to be misunderstood or even persecuted for praying publicly. As with all prayer, public prayer should be offered with the correct attitude and motive. From several scriptural examples comes a clear picture of acceptable and God-honoring public prayer.

Hannah, the mother of the prophet Samuel, was childless for years, enduring the shame and persecution that childlessness brought to Jewish women in Bible times (see 1 Sam. 1:1-6). She went regularly to the temple to beseech God to provide her with a child and prayed fervently out of "great anguish and grief." So heartfelt was her prayer that Eli, the priest, perceived her as coming drunk to the house of the Lord.

"So Hannah arose after they had finished eating and drinking in Shiloh. Now Eli the priest was sitting on the seat by the doorpost of the tabernacle of the Lord. And she was in bitterness of soul, and prayed to the Lord and wept in anguish. Then she made a vow and said, "O Lord of hosts, if You will indeed look on the affliction of Your maidservant and remember me, and not forget Your maidservant, but will give Your maidservant a male child, then I will give him to the Lord all the days of his life, and no razor shall come upon his head." And it happened, as she continued praying before the Lord, that Eli watched her mouth. Now Hannah spoke in her heart; only her lips moved, but her voice was not heard. Therefore Eli thought she was drunk. So Eli said to her, "How long will you be drunk? Put your wine away from you!" But Hannah answered and said, "No, my lord, I am a woman of sorrowful spirit. I have drunk neither wine nor intoxicating drink, but have poured out my soul before the Lord." (1 Sam. 1:9-15)

Here is an example of public prayer being misinterpreted. Hannah's prayer was righteous, and her heart was in the right place. She was not trying to draw attention to herself, but was simply distraught and overwhelmed with the need to pray. Eli thought she was drunk, but that was his mistake, not her sin.

Daniel's public prayer presented an opportunity for his enemies to persecute him and attempt to have him killed. Daniel excelled in his duties as one of the administrators under King Darius to such a degree that the king was contemplating making him head over all the kingdom (see Dan. 6:1-3). This infuriated the other administrators, and they looked for a way to discredit or destroy Daniel. They encouraged Darius to issue a decree forbidding his subjects from praying to anyone other than the king for the next thirty days. The penalty for disobeying was to be thrown into a den of lions. Daniel, however, continued to pray so openly to God that he could be seen at his bedroom window doing so. Daniel prayed in a way that not only was visible to others, but exposed him to his enemies. However, he clearly knew that God was honored by his prayer, so he didn't give up his custom. He didn't put the opinions and even the threats of men above his desire to obey the Lord above all.

In Matthew 6:5-7, Jesus gives two ways to ensure that our prayers are righteous. First, prayers should not be for the purpose of being seen by others as righteous or "spiritual." Second, prayers should be authentic, as from the heart, and not just vain repetition or "empty phrases." However, when compared with other Scriptures that show people praying in public, we know that this is not an exhortation to always pray alone. The issue is to avoid sin. Those who struggle with the desire to be seen as righteous and who notice that temptation creeping in during public prayer would do well to heed Jesus' prescription to get alone and pray just to the Father, who will reward in secret. Jesus knew that the Pharisees' desire was to be seen by men as righteous, not to talk to God. This statement about prayer was meant to convict and is instructive for all Christians, but it does not mean that all prayer must be secret. Public prayer should be God-honoring, selfless, and based in a true desire to speak to God and not to men. If we pray publicly without violating these principles, we do well to pray publicly. If, however, our conscience forbids it, there is nothing less effective about a prayer offered in secret.

Pray While Crying and Others Are Joyfully Shouting

God can somehow blend crying and joyful shouting together, as He did in Ezra and Nehemiah's days, when the temple was being rededicated. It was impossible to distinguish between the sound of those who shouted and those who wept.

When I first came to the Lord it was at the very tail end of a great spiritual tsunami wave known as the Charismatic Renewal. In this great awakening, I saw so many victories, experienced so much joy and saw God do so many miracles and great things even in my own life. Unintentionally, I became very critical of people who prayed with sorrow and tears. I thought they did not understand God's word, and therefore, they were not living in the victory. I thought they needed a good old fashioned lecture about having more faith or perhaps they needed to get in the prayer line at church to ask God for a powerful, prophetic word by the visiting preacher. It took me a very long time to "get it", to understand it completely, but I finally realized what they were truly going through when God allowed me to go through my very own tearful times in life. I quickly learned that all people needed was to pour out their hearts to God. Through sad, mad, or in glad times there is no shame in praying with tears. When people in the Bible prayed with tears, God didn't tell them to go home and dry their tears and come back when they were happy and full of faith again. He met them right there in the midst of their sorrow and tears and led them to victory.

Pray Short Prayers Or Long Prayers

Have you ever sought God at the start of the day for only about fifteen to thirty minutes, and then lived all day under condemnation because the devil told you your prayer was too short, that you should have prayed for an hour? Short prayers are just as honorable and effective as long prayers. The shortest prayer that Peter prayed was, "Lord, save me!" However it got Jesus' attention and immediate answer.

"And Peter answered Him and said, 'Lord, if it is You, command me to come to You on the water.' So He said, 'Come.' And when Peter had come down out of the boat, he walked on the water to go to Jesus. But when he saw that the wind was boisterous, he was afraid; and beginning to sink he cried out, saying, 'Lord, save me!' And immediately Jesus stretched out His hand and caught him..." (Matt. 14:28-31)

The shortest prayer I ever prayed was when I was in the red rock mountains of Sedona, Arizona with a cute girlfriend of mine. I was jumping, standing, and sitting on the edge of a 40 ft. tall mountain cliff showing off to this pretty girl, when all of a sudden, the soft, brittle ground of the edge of the cliff gave way!

THE PRAYER ANOINTING

I lost my balance and started to fall straight down the mountainside. As I began to fall, I was headed toward two sharp, jagged boulders which would have been to my demise. At that moment, all I could pray was, "Jesus!" And as if God had sent a heavenly angel to bear me up at that exact moment I cried out, I was somehow supernaturally nudged in mid-air to the very center of those two jagged boulders where there was soft sand where I ultimately landed. I only walked away with a bruised heel on my right foot (and a bruised ego). I should have hit those sharp rocks and split my head wide open, or broke my back and become paralyzed, or worse; I could have died that day. It was a very short prayer, but it brought about the miracle that saved and preserved my life for years to come.

There are times when long prayers are appropriate for the time and place. Several years ago, I was asked to preach in a church, in Texas. When I got up to preach the spirit of prayer came upon me, and I prayed for more than an hour. Through that one hour of prayer, the Spirit of the Lord broke a tremendous force that was binding, blinding and preventing the Spirit to flow in that church. Everything I prayed made sense because I was praying by the anointing.

Pray With Fasting
Fasting can be for:
1. A meal or two.
2. A day or two.
3. A week or two.
4. A month or longer.

Jesus prayed and fasted for forty days; not to gain knowledge, but to present Himself to the Father as an instrument ready to do His will. In the same way, we should also pray and fast to prepare ourselves as instruments, ready to do the Father's will.

Pray In Jesus' Name

It makes no difference how you pray, when you pray, or from what posture or position you pray, as long as you pray in Jesus' name. We do not pray in the name of the church. We do not pray in the name of righteousness. The only name we pray in is the mighty name of Jesus Christ.

Positions Of Prayer

The positions I am talking about are not physical positions, such as kneeling at the altar. Kneeling hurts some people's knees, due to physical limitations, they simply cannot do this. The positions I am talking about are these:

1. Sitting at Jesus' feet (see Luke 8:35).
2. Coming before the throne or as before a judge (Heb. 4:16).
3. Standing before the mirror of the perfect law of liberty (see James 1:25).

Sitting At Jesus' Feet

Isaiah 52:7 KJV says, "How beautiful upon the mountains are the feet of him that bringeth good tidings, that publisheth peace; that bringeth good tidings of good, that publisheth salvation; that saith unto Zion, Thy God reigneth!" Those are the feet that were, no doubt, fondly caressed by an adoring mother in the manger and pitter-pattered around the carpenter shop. Those were the feet that were supposed to follow the family from the temple, but stayed with the leaders. They stepped into Jordan at baptism and would later walk atop the water. They stood on the mount preaching, walked a thousand miles helping, and ran to the hurting. They kicked over the tables of those who made His house a mockery. Those feet shook off dust from places which rejected Him, but moved on to another place! To walk beside them, for a privileged few must have felt like walking on air! A tender blade of grass so green crushed in the footstep of the Nazarene, springs back and waves a message to a bird as it sings, "That's Him!" They didn't run when His accusers approached, but rather they walked up the hill to Golgotha and were nailed to a cross, but in so being those bruised heels stomped on the head of the serpent...a crushing victory! They descended below the earth and led captivity captive...then those feet walked out of that tomb, walked the road to Emmaus with His disciples, and showed all His followers how they can walk with Him after His departure. Then they left the ground at His ascension just as ours will at His return, and then we can join Him seven years later when those glorious feet will once again touchdown in the end zone of life on Earth as He proclaims, "I'm back to set up my Kingdom!" What a privilege it is that we today (and every day of our lives), are able to sit at the feet of Jesus! There we will find:

1. A Place of Pardon
   Luke 7:38 "And stood at His feet behind Him weeping, and began to wash His feet with tears, and did wipe them with the hairs of her head, and kissed His feet, and anointed them with the ointment". In humility this woman, void of chastity, found forgiveness from her sins as she knelt at the feet of Jesus. The Lord allowed this woman who had made a living from impure contact to touch Him...and His virtue became her own as her faith and repentance were expressed there at His feet! Or another, taken in the very act of adultery; Jesus didn't condemn her, He forgave her, and put her accusers to shame in the process, then charging her to go and sin no more!

2. A Place of Healing

   Matthew 15:30 "And great multitudes came unto Him, having with them those that were lame, blind, dumb, maimed, and many others, and cast them down at Jesus' feet; and He healed them." Outcasts and rejects find their happy place at His feet. When you pray, look into His face through the eyes of faith. How that can build you up; creating humility and confidence! Let your mind think, "He is looking at me; I am looking at Him." It is a mental and spiritual position. Jesus said of Mary, who chose the position of sitting at His feet and looking into His face, that she had chosen the greater part.

Coming Before The Throne Or As Before A Judge

When one approaches a judge in a courtroom, there is a specific protocol to follow and to be observed. If you have an appointment with a judge and you go into the courtroom all primed to tell him that you wanted a jury trial and you hurry down the aisle through the door to speak to him about it, the judge will jump up and strike the podium with his gavel and say to you, "Stop, back up and get on the other side of that rail where you belong, or I will throw you in jail right now for contempt of court!" You do not approach the judge's bench in his or her courtroom unless a request is made with the proper protocol being followed; and only then could the permission be granted or not be granted. When we come before God's throne – when we come to Him as the just judge – He tells us just the opposite; He tells us to come boldly. There are no gates, no rails, no one standing guard to throw us into jail. We are invited to come boldly to the throne of grace and speak our petitions.

"Seeing then that we have a great High Priest who has passed through the heavens, Jesus the Son of God, let us hold fast our confession. For we do not have a High Priest who cannot sympathize with our weaknesses, but was in all points tempted as we are, yet without sin. Let us therefore come boldly to the throne of grace, that we may obtain mercy and find grace to help in time of need." (Heb. 4:14-16)

When we come to the throne of the heavenly judge we are talking to the Anointed One. When we pray, we are talking to the Chief Justice of all judges. When our position is that of appearing before God's throne, our prayers consist of presenting our rights according to the covenant. We stand before God and say, "God, You said that You are my healer; now I want to know why I am not healed. You said You are my deliverer; I want to know when my deliverance is coming." If that seems too bold, just remember that your rights come because of your relationship to God. You come before the judge on legal grounds alone and you claim only what is written in the Word of God. Because the Word says that God is our healer, you can say to God, "You promised to heal me, why hasn't it been done?"

My spiritual father went through his Bible and literally wrote his name beside several hundred verses. Sometimes he would leave the Bible open and say to the prosecuting attorney (the devil), "Every time you come into this courtroom, notice that this verse is for me." The Book of Hebrews says that Jesus is the High Priest of our profession. In the Greek, *profession* means "to say the same thing that He says." God wants us to say the same thing about ourselves, about the enemy, and about other people, that the Word says. When some people hear that someone is sick, they say, "They brought it upon themselves." Or "They are going to die." When I hear that someone is sick, I say, "The Lord is going to heal them." Why do I say that? Because the Lord (The Lion of Judah) said, "Go tell it (roar it) from the mountains, in

133

the valleys, and from the rooftops. I have come to deliver everyone from all their destructions."

Standing Before The Mirror The Perfect Law Of Liberty
Prayer helps us remember who we are. We look at our problems, and according to what we see with our own vision, they become mountains, and we become smaller and smaller. But, when we go to prayer, and we look at the Lord in the law of liberty, the mountains start shrinking, and we appear larger. Because the reflection of Christ in the mirror is greater, we are no longer touched by words of criticism, condemnation, rejection, and the experience of isolation. We come from the position of standing before that mirror saying, "I am a King's Kid; the offspring of the Great Lion King. His Kingly blood flows through my veins. I am more than a conqueror. I am a conquering lion – king of my jungle. I know what I am saying because I know what His Word says. I am anointed to roar!"

Chapter 9
Esther: Appointed and Anointed

A Type Of The Disadvantaged

Perhaps the best way to view the story of Esther (for the purpose of this study) is to start at the end rather than in the beginning. Because of Esther's strategic placement (her appointment) in history and the Spirit of God (the anointing) working in her life, multitudes of Jews were saved from death. What a marvelous use of the anointing! What a worthy cause to justify God's special appointment of Esther! As we have already seen in the life of Samson, and as we shall see in each Biblical character we examine, both God's appointment and His anointing are to accomplish His purposes. In both Old and New Testaments, those whom God appointed, He also anointed; the two are inseparable. When God calls us to a ministry, a position, or a job, He equips us to function in that role. "Faithful is He that calleth you, who also will do it." "...that he which hath begun a good work in you will perform it until the day of Jesus Christ" (see Phil. 1:6 KJV). He begins it with the appointment, the call; He accomplishes it through the anointing, the working of His Spirit.

The historical setting for Esther's story is the Persian Empire at the height of its prominence in about the 5th century B.C. The most common date is 465-486 B.C. The Empire included 127 provinces stretching from India to Ethiopia. The Persians treated most of the conquered kingdoms, including Judah and Israel, with exceptional lenience. Subjected peoples were allowed to worship their own gods and keep their own customs. Thus, Esther and her uncle Mordecai would have worshipped Jehovah and maintained their Jewish identity. They would have been aware of their history as a people set apart to God, a people with a diverse purpose, a people who had, time after time, experienced deliverance by the mighty hand of their God. As we briefly consider the events that lead to the preservation of God's people and the destruction of their enemies in Esther's time, a pattern emerges both of God's appointment of people to serve His purposes and His anointing them with wisdom, favor and courage. (It would benefit you to read the entire book of Esther.) In the opening chapters, the king is searching for a new queen because the former queen, Vashti, has been banished from his presence due to her disobedience. The call has gone out to all the provinces that young, beautiful virgins are to be selected and brought to the king's palace and placed in his harem under the care of Hegai, a eunuch. One of these young women, Esther, at the instruction of her uncle Mordecai, does not reveal her Jewish heritage. There is something about Esther that catches the attention of Hegai; she pleased him and found favor with him. Esther received special care and consideration, special food and beauty treatments, and the best place in the harem. Esther won the favor of everyone who saw her. After the required twelve months of beauty treatments and instruction for these young women, the time came when they were taken, one-by-one, to the king. When it was Esther's turn, she won the king's favor and approval over all the other women, and she became the new queen. If the story ended here, it would be one of those "the Princess found her Prince Charming – a happily ever after" ending, but God did not appoint and anoint Esther so she could have a good life with position, prosperity and prestige. His purposes were on a much grander scale. Esther was appointed and anointed for the benefit of others.

As the story progresses, the villain, Haman, comes on the scene. Haman is elevated to a seat of honor higher than all the king's nobles. At the king's command, people were to kneel down and pay honor to Haman, but Mordecai would not bow down. Haman was enraged when he was told that Mordecai would not honor him. When he learned that Mordecai was a Jew, he determined to not only have Mordecai killed, but also to destroy all Jews throughout the entire kingdom of King Xerxes. So Haman goes to the king, and with carefully chosen words, describes these certain people scattered in all the provinces whose customs are different from those of other people, and who do not obey the king's laws. He tells the king that it is not in his best interest to tolerate them, and asks that a decree be issued to destroy them. He even offers to pay the wages of the men who will carry out this business. The king agrees, and the official order is sent to all the provinces. The order is to destroy, kill and annihilate all Jews young and old, women and children in a single day (the thirteenth day of the twelfth month) and to plunder their goods. When the edict was issued in Susa where Esther and Mordecai were, Mordecai learned of it. He tore his clothes, put on sackcloth and ashes, and went out into the city, wailing loudly and bitterly. Esther was told about Mordecai, and she was greatly distressed. She sent a messenger to find out what was troubling him. Mordecai told the messenger why he was so troubled and sent Esther a copy of the edict ordering the annihilation of the Jews. He said to tell Esther to go into the king's presence and beg for mercy and plead with him for her people. Esther sent word back to Mordecai, reminding him that it was common knowledge that no one could approach the king in the inner court without being summoned; if they did, the law was clear: they would be put to death. The only exception was if the king extended the gold scepter to that person and spared his life. Esther said she had not been called to go to the king for thirty days. Mordecai's answer to Esther was blunt and unequivocal: "And Mordecai told them to answer Esther: 'Do not think in your heart that you will escape in the king's palace any more than all the other Jews. For if you remain completely silent at this time, relief and deliverance will arise for the Jews from another place, but you and your father's house will perish. Yet who knows whether you have come to the kingdom for such a time as this?'" (Esther 4:13-14)

Truly, Esther was appointed to the kingdom for such a time, and she was anointed with courage, wisdom, grace and favor. Esther's story is one of God's faithfulness, God's provision, and God's intervention in the affairs of nations through the vessels He has chosen and equipped. It is a story that can provoke us to believe God, to commit ourselves wholly to His keeping, to rejoice in our place of service, and to expect His Holy Spirit to equip us for whatever lies ahead. It will always be this way in the Kingdom of God. We see it all throughout the O.T. We see it in the N.T., and we now have God's written assurance that all who believe in Jesus Christ are both set apart (appointed) and equipped (anointed) for His purposes, and have been called to become a mighty voice for God (appointed and anointed to roar)!

Esther's Anointing
Esther's anointing will bring a person from the status of a slave, with no rights at all to a position of sitting on the throne and possessing as much as half the Kingdom. It gives an advantage to those who are down and out, and can see no light at the end of the tunnel. In this lesson, we are reflecting on the measure of the anointing and the many ways it was manifested in Esther's life; I

call this the "upper-hand-anointing." In these teachings on Esther's anointing, Samson's anointing, Aaron's anointing and David's anointing, I use the title to refer to how the anointing functioned, and the unction of the Holy Spirit worked in their lives. The anointing did not belong to them, but they were supernaturally endowed with a special power, grace, and favor to complete their kingdom calling and to fulfill God's divine will in the earth. The book of Esther is filled with many spiritual gems. All of Esther's victories were a direct result of the anointing in her life. Without the anointing, Esther would have died as a slave. This anointing can come to us today by the Word. Reading the Word, praying the Word and confessing the Word exposes us to the anointing; the flow of life in Jesus Christ, the Anointed One. Our objective, when hearing the Word preached, should not be to judge the speaker, but to hear and comprehend the Word. Neither should our objective be entertainment or inspiration. I get inspired at football games and by tear-jerking movies, but this and many other similar things that inspire us are not inspiration; they are nothing more than emotion and enthusiasm. Our obligation when the Word is preached is to listen and then ask ourselves, "What does it mean to me?" What the preacher is saying may not always have the same meaning to me as it does to them because every Word of God purifies at least seven different ways in the furnaces of earth. So we can say there are at least seven different dimensions of Biblical application for edification.

The words of the Lord are pure, Like silver tried in a furnace of earth, purified seven times. You shall keep them, O Lord, You shall preserve them from this generation forever. (Ps. 12:6-7)

In addition, when we hear the Word being preached, our objective should never be to poke our wife or husband at church

139

or a conference and say, "What are you getting out of this?" We should say, "Lord, what do you have in this for me?" Don't feel guilty when your mind goes down one channel of thought and the preacher goes down another. Don't feel like the preacher is wrong, and you are right, or you are wrong, and the preacher is right. Just realize that God is a multi-versed God, who can speak to everyone at one time through one voice. Everyone can hear His Word and apply it to their situation, at their level of knowledge and maturity; that is if they are not in a critical or judgmental state, or have a closed-door attitude. When we close the door on the Word, the anointing cannot be ministered into our spirits. Another thing we should not say is, "Oh, I've heard that before." The repetition of a truth aids the implementation of that truth in our hearts. It is not the truth that is in the mind, but the truth that is in the heart that causes the hands to act, the feet to walk, and the mind to think. So do not disqualify truth that you have heard before, but let it speak to you again and again. There are texts that I have found helpful all my life, day after day. The Word of God is a living oracle sent to give us abundant life. So when we hear the Word, we should ask ourselves, "Am I practicing this Word- not only in church, but also at school, home and on the job? Do I choose to practice the Word when I am in a bad mood, or just when I am in a good mood?" All these factors contribute to the effect of the anointing in your life. The anointing, the oil of the Spirit, comes to us through the Word, prayer, praise, the prophetic word, edification, and the returning of good for evil.

Zechariah 4 speaks of the two anointed ones, who symbolically are pictured as olive trees standing by the Lord of Hosts for the purpose of allowing oil to come into the lamps. The lamps are the lamps of the world. Jesus said, "You are the lamps (lights) of the world" (see Matt. 5:14). We are the lamps that are to be full of His light, but we have to be full of oil. We need both oil and fire. Without oil, fire cannot be sustained; it will not last past the flash of the church service or the prophetic conference. In order for the fire to stay and be a light day after day, you have to be full of the anointing oil. I have learned to get something out of any message that is preached, because I expose myself to the Word, and not necessarily to the instrument bringing the message. No message carrier is perfect in all knowledge. No one is developed in all experience, and no one has seen everything from all seven directions of a divine dimension.

During one of the services at Desert Rose Community Church, while getting ready to go up and preach, I was sitting on the edge of my seat like a track runner – muscles quivering, ready to go. The Lord said, "What are you doing?" I answered, "I'm getting ready to go up to the pulpit." He said, "With what attitude are you getting ready to go?" I answered, "I've got to keep this church in control. I've got to keep this ministry going. I'm ready to move in the Spirit." He said, "You cannot move in the anointing with that attitude. You can use your own excitement; you can huff and puff, and push and pull; but the flow of the Spirit will not be there. You must trust Me and rest in faith." I did not realize I was not resting in faith. He said, "You must trust." I did not realize I was not trusting, but I committed the remainder of the service to the Lord, and I was able to come to rest, and to trust. That is how many of us are. We become tense, uptight, and up in the air. I have known people who cannot even get dressed to go to church without getting upset because they are under so much pressure. I have known other people (they travel fairly often) who tell me that every time they prepare to go on a trip their whole day is ruined because of the stress of packing and all the other things they have to do in order to go.

We do not receive all the anointing oil in salvation. We do not receive all of the anointing in the baptism of the Holy Spirit. We receive it from degree to degree, measure to measure, here a little, there a little, a cupful at a time, from experience to experience. Isaiah 28:9-10 says, "Whom will he teach knowledge? And whom will he make to understand the message? Those just weaned from milk? Those just drawn from the breasts? For precept must be upon precept, precept upon precept, line upon line, line upon line, here a little, there a little." Romans 5 teaches us that as we experience trials and tribulations, we develop patience so that we have joy and rejoicing in all our circumstances. This gives us the upper hand.

Meditate On The Word
For many years, I would listen to tapes or CD's of my own sermons to meditate and find out what the Holy Spirit was saying. Then I discovered that I wasn't practicing a lot of what I had just roared out to the congregation. Now, before you judge me too quickly here, I think that if we are all honest with ourselves, including us anointed preachers, we will admit that it is a lot easier to say something than it is to execute it. Jesus said it is not he who hears the Word and rejoices in it, but it is he who hears and practices the word is wise (see Matt. 7:24). I also learned the value of the printed page. With it, you can not only meditate and go over the material again and again, but you can also use it for practicing spiritual principles. This teaching about Esther's anointing will help us to gain the upper hand in many areas of our lives. Meditating on the Word of God will also bring us to a place where we can release everything to God on a moment-by-moment basis.

Prayer and Praise

We are exposed to the anointing through prayer – praying in the Spirit – and through singing songs or singing in the Spirit. That is why we must constantly attend church. Some people think the only reason why pastors tell people they should be in church on Sunday morning, Sunday night, Wednesday night, and go to prayer meetings and Bible study, is because we just want to build up our numbers and receive an offering. Numbers of filled seats, numbers of bills in the offering plate, and the numbers of knees bowed at the altar are not the equivalent and measure of success in God's eyes. The truth is, praying or singing in the Spirit is only helpful when you receive something from the anointing that breaks the yoke. Just singing songs with no yoke being broken, just kneeling and going through prayer is not enough to make the manifested presence of God known. Many people look and talk like Christians (look and act like lions), but when the battle comes, they flee in every direction, hiding from the voice that speaks from the most excellent glory (flee at the ferocious sound of the Lion of Judah's roar), that is shaking the heavens and the earth. They look for some place to escape from the penetrating light of the Word as it is preached. Why? They are not absorbing the anointing.

When light finds oil, there is a fire that brings holy joy to the soul. However when light finds no oil, there is a scorching and a burning, and we say, "The words coming forth from the pastor are harsh. They should have been said in a different way." The truth is, in earlier days of the Charismatic Revival, no one cared how loud their voices were, or how harsh or sweet they were, and no one cared about how the preacher structured his sermons. Why? They were too busy absorbing the anointing like a sponge. They were walking and living in the Spirit. When you are walking and living in the Spirit, singing in the Spirit, and praying in the Spirit – not with your own agenda, but with the Lord's agenda- there is a release and an overflowing of the anointing. God is finding people who are disadvantaged, and He is saying, "I'm going to do a new thing – not on the basis of how many thousands have been praying, but on the basis of who can hear Me; the sound of My roar while being in a position of disadvantage." In Isaiah 10 KJV it says the Assyrians, Egyptians and Babylonians are going to have a rod (which represents rule). Verse 27 states, "And it shall come to pass in that day, that his burden shall be taken away from off thy shoulder…" (The burden was a force controlling their lives). Most people want to be less controlled by their circumstances and have more spiritual control. Our circumstances should not control our joy. What other people do should not control our peace. What we have seen in the past should not be the basis for our faith in the future. Our joy, peace and faith should be based upon what we hear of the voice of the Lord in our spirit.

The picture and the story in the book of Esther are of Israel under God's correction. In earlier times, we would have said that Israel was being judged. Today, we are more careful because people don't understand the Biblical use of the word *judged*. Some people think of judgment as God cutting them off, but God was not cutting Israel off – not in any way, shape or form. He was correcting them. Today, the church in America is being corrected. Today, the nation is being corrected. Our economy is being corrected. The practice of spending before you get is evil. It is violent, godless, and corrupt for a government to put two and three generations in debt by trillions of dollars just to keep the system afloat. God is judging the system; He is correcting and redirecting our course of action. In the midst of the restoration when the people were rebuilding the temple, the pillars and the beautiful entryway of Solomon's temple, they discovered they were not doing most of their rebuilding according to the Word of God. They were not rebuilding according to the pattern; they were doing it according to their own will. People are still doing that today, but all over the world God is correcting, restoring and bringing the church to a place where we will listen to His directions. We need new direction in our family relationships. We need God's direction restored to our personal finances and in every area of our lives. We need restoration of our faith walk. We have practically made faith nothing more than "blab it and grab it, name it and claim it." There is so much more to faith than that.

The people in Esther's day, just like many today who have not studied God's Word and said, "Let us do it God's way," were, and are, placed in situations of disadvantage. Esther was in exile; she was not in her own land. She was not under her own roof, and she was not under her own authority. She would not claim her own consulate because there was none. She had no representative in the courts of that kingdom whatsoever. She had absolutely nothing but God; her position was one of disadvantage. In fact, she was a slave. She was actually a trophy of war placed into the King's harem. She was the most attractive young lady in the harem and the king kept her to parade around at his parties. She was in the most disadvantaged position, one in which she could have had her head cut off at the whim of the king. Her life and any of the other's lives could end if anything about them displeased the king. The king seemed to be a just and fair man, but he had just appointed Haman (an evil and corrupt man who was very energetic and very desiring of his own will) to a position that could bring harm not only to Esther, but to all Jews in the kingdom. Yet, we find later that she found favor with those who had influence and she was elevated to queendom. Esther seemed to have only one advantage at first. Her uncle Mordecai had been received by the king as a cupbearer, but a cupbearer, who is a servant, could not go into the king with a request. He could only go in and say, "Sir, bless you..." and leave. He could not request anything, so he was of no hope or help to her in her situation at that time. Her life would go down the drain unless there were an anointing at work in her heart. God will deal with us and bring us into disadvantaged situations where we cannot exercise our own will and stir our own emotions. We must find a flow of the anointing that will ease us, release us, and reveal the way. Zechariah 4:6 KJV says, "We are going to make it through not by might, nor by power, but by My Spirit, saith the Lord of hosts." When I think of this passage in Zechariah, I am reminded of a long-time friend of mine named Ed Norman. Brother Ed ministers the Word of God from his wheelchair. He is paralyzed from the neck down, yet, since he received the anointing in his life he has had the upper hand. Although it seems by appearance, that he is one of the most disadvantaged individuals you could ever meet; it is that very appearance, empowered by the anointing, by which he can communicate to disadvantaged people that very few of us could ever reach.

Esther needed an anointing for the power to be released from the king's harem. The second was when Haman became jealous of Esther's uncle Mordecai and discovered he was a Jew. He had gallows on which to hang Mordecai. As soon as Haman launched his battle against Mordecai and increased the scope of the battle to include all the Jews in the provinces of Persia, the anointing that was on Esther began to reveal God's plan for deliverance. At this point, the king did not know that his newly acquired wife, Esther, was also a Jew. As for Esther, she was now in more danger than she ever was when she was in the king's harem. She was now in a position where, if anything happened, she would have to be delivered by the hand of the Almighty God. Esther was in a position from which only God could deliver her, just as many of us are today. First, we must have insight to what the problems and dangers are that we are facing. Second, we must have a system, method, and a plan in place. Esther was given a plan of deliverance for her nation. No matter what situation we are in or what situation we might someday find ourselves in, God has promised us, His people, restoration. In Jeremiah, He told the children of Israel "I will send you into Babylon, and you will be there seventy years; after that, I will bring you back." That promise stood over Esther as well as it stood over Daniel. It said: "Your nation is not going to be wiped out. Your ministry is not going to come to an end, but a new beginning, and in your coming out, the glory will be greater than before your captivity." We all have these promises. Yes, we will all go through trials, but we will come out of them, and when we come out, we will come out sitting on thrones with kings, holding the rod of authority and righteousness, and ruling as kings.We are lion kings ruling our domain like unto our father 'The Lion King' of Judah. So, in her authority, Esther put on her royal robes. One is the robe of righteousness; God gives everyone the gift of righteousness. We should glory in the fact that righteousness is a gift and the anointing operates in our lives by the same measure that we receive the energizing of faith, hope and love.

We have the choice to think of ourselves according to who we are in the flesh, with the ragged, dirty clothes of outward appearances and negative thinking, or we can choose to think on the Lord, who takes care of all of it, removes all of it, washes all of it away, and who covers us with His righteousness. You can put on your robe of righteousness when your carnal nature flares up and says, "This problem will never be settled." With your robe of righteousness on, your problem can be dealt with. You will, ultimately, get rid of it – in death – if you can die to self

147

through the Word, through prayer, praise, and through witnessing. Doing so will bring death to pride and self-life. You can die to self here and now by releasing the anointing in bad times. Instead of saying, "That old self is there forever, and faith doesn't work." Take your robe of righteousness, and say, "By this robe I am more than a conqueror! I am a lion king - king of the jungle of my self-life!"

The second robe is the robe of salvation, which means deliverance. The deliverance is for the spirit, the soul and the body. It makes no difference whether it is an emotional need (fleshly), a faith need (spiritual), or a physical need (body). God says, "I will cover you with a garment." As Esther began to think on what she has in her possession that would give her favor in the king's eyes, she realized her royal garments were a gift of the king. There is no doubt that as she meditates upon this fact, faith arose in her heart. Wherever there is faith, there is an anointing. God has plenty of time scheduled into His plan, for Jeremiah the prophet said, "You will be there seventy years undergoing changes necessary to make you the man or woman of God that He intends you to be." When Israel was in the wilderness, God set aside forty years. The forty years was the set time to bring them out of bondage. The seventy years with Esther, in her time, was to set God's people on the throne and put them into an influential role.

The third garment is the robe of praise. Esther put on the garment of praise, and we are also called to do the same. I can remember back when I was a teenager, how the Spirit anointed me to sing praises while I was doing menial chores that I hated, such as cleaning up the backyard, or pulling out overgrown weeds in between the landscaping rocks in the front yard of my parent's home. Likewise, all of us, as we grow more in grace, we will find those difficult places the Spirit likes to deal with, but as we allow the Spirit to work in those places, more filth and bondage is flushed out of our lives. This will drive us to our knees in prayer, seeking deliverance. In time, we learn that all bondage comes from the flesh and all liberty comes from the Spirit, for which reason we are admonished to put on the clothing of righteousness, peace and joy in the Holy Spirit. We do not teach eradication of the sin nature – we teach conquering it with beautiful garments while waiting on the redemption. The King James Version describes that as, "The purchased possession," which speaks of our carnal bodies. There is no good thing in my flesh, said Paul in Philippians 3:3, "...rejoice in Christ Jesus, and have no confidence in the flesh," and in Romans 7:18, "For I know that in me (that is, in my flesh) nothing good dwells."

Putting on your garment of praise always gives you the advantage. Of course, the enemy will try to prevent you from praising by telling you that you cannot praise, or that there is no logical reason why you should praise in this particular circumstance or situation. Maybe you are in a situation now where you have had to fight off the thoughts that say there is no logical reason to praise God. If you will rise up in the Spirit and put on your garments and say, "I will experience deliverance because these are my garments; I am going to wear them no matter what anyone thinks or says about it!" Whenever I go somewhere, I like to wear clothes that fit the occasion. Nothing is worse than to go into a particular church meeting or function underdressed or overdressed. Whenever I am asked to go minister in a church for the first time, I like to learn some particulars from the Senior Pastor or the church staff prior to arriving. First, I find out what their church background and culture is like, and secondly, how they dress on Sunday morning and Wednesday night services. I have gone to minister in churches a couple times where I was overdressed. I came from a church culture and background that expected the preacher to show up wearing his best Sunday suit, tie, and matching handkerchief. I have shown up to churches to preach where the Senior Pastor, his staff, and the congregation came to church wearing modern jeans with holes, cut off shorts, t-shirts, and flip-flop sandals for shoes. However, I have also gone to minister in a few churches underdressed because I did not know their church customs, and I am not accustomed to wearing a Three- Piece Suit, and clerical robes, to preach in either. When I come to church, I don't want to come questioning, doubting and wondering about what people look like and dress like in the congregation. I want to come clothed with my garments of praise, and praise God for everyone in the church, regardless of their situation, suits, or sandals.

"And they heard the voice of the Lord God walking in the garden in the cool of the day..." (Gen. 3:8). The Hebrew says, "God breathed and His voice was heard in their spirit." God imparted into Adam part of His mind, giving him an advantage over his enemies. The book of Revelation describes the voice of God as the sound of many waters – the sound of thunder – the sound of multitudes praising God. I am going to start glorying in the gift of righteousness by putting it on as a garment. I am as righteous as I can ever be. You must do the same. I also have another garment in my spiritual closet – the garment of salvation. You have it, too. Take it out, put it on, and identify who you are in Christ. I remember singing the old song, "I'm saved, saved, saved, through His power divine" and other songs about salvation. When I would sing them, my whole being would tremble and shake under the power of the reality that I am saved. Put on the garment of praise and say, "I am going to bless the Lord at all times. His praise shall continually be in my mouth."

When I find murmuring and complaining, I put my praise garment over them. When I find doubt and fear, I put my praise garment over them. I don't go into a ten-year ordeal of trying to dig out the root of fear or doubt. I put on the garment, and the garment gives me a new self, a new identity. I am, inwardly, what Gods garments make me outwardly. Many people try to clean up their carnality – their outward person – before they put on the garments that give them their identity. The identity gives us the authority to clean up the carnality.

There is another robe or garment that Esther put on. In Ephesians 6, we discover that the anointing is applied to our lives through wearing the garment of warfare. Esther's battles were more like our battles than were David's and Samson's. Their battles were with the Philistines, who symbolized the impulses, drives and lusts of the flesh. Esther's battles were fought in the courtroom, where wisdom and truth prevail. When Ephesians 6:13 says, "… and having done all, to stand." It doesn't indicate David with his slingshot and stones knocking down the giant, then taking his own sword and cutting off his head, while proclaiming "My enemy is dead." The description is a legal claim – from the head covering (the hope of salvation) – to the feet (the shoes of the gospel of peace). Each garment gives the believer the needed identity for the judge to make a favorable decision in the quest to obtain our inheritance.

The Helmet – The Hope Of Salvation
This helmet pertains to the salvation of the mind. Salvation is, therefore, worked out by the renewing of the mind. Romans 12:2 says, "…but be transformed by the renewing of your mind…" Salvation is worked into us through the renewing of our mind.

The minute I see something wrong in my life, I don't hide it, I take it to the judge who is the author and finisher of my faith, and confess it. Some Christians believe they don't have to confess their sins. To the contrary; a Christian must confess his or her sins – not as a penitent sinner, but as a victorious believer, confessing that sin has arisen within the dominion of the King and that sin shall not have dominion. The presence of that sin – the presence of the enemy – is not a sign that we have sold out or that we are traitors. Neither is it a sign that we are weak Christians or that, at long last, our secret sins are exposed. Rather, the presence of sin has appeared as a challenge against God's truth, not our experience. It challenges His truth which said, "If the Son therefore shall make you free, ye shall be free indeed." (John 8:36 KJV)

The presence of sin rises to say, "You are not free. You feel this, you want that. The emotion of sin is in your members." The Spirit abides with the anointing to continue to say to us, "But if I do that which I would not, it is not I, it is sin dwelling in my members; it is a separate entity other than me, a born again believer. It is a thing condemned, but I am not condemned, sin is condemned. The motion of sin is condemned. The presence of sin is condemned. It is not condemned, though, by a fresh crucifixion; it is condemned by a fresh release of the anointing to demonstrate that, in the presence of my enemies, God has spread a table before me. When it looks like I am falling, I cannot fail, for underneath me are the everlasting arms. When it looks like I have fallen so far that every bone will be broken, suddenly I am standing upright on my feet, and my teeth have not even been jarred in my mouth because I landed so softly in the graceful hands of the Redeemer. I realize sin is no longer my enemy. Sin comes to dethrone the Christ, not me. My sins once brought Him from His throne to the cross. The cross took Him back to the throne. My sins can never bring Him off the throne. "His cross is able to deliver me from all sin!"

By the anointing, we put on a helmet of hope, and when we do, we release more anointing. When emotions of sin arise in my members, I say, "I don't discount my victory by your challenge." If someone comes by my house and challenges my ownership of it, I take out my deed, title and loan papers and say, "I'm a witness, the deed is a witness, and the bank is a witness. They have my signature; I am the one responsible." Sometimes the enemy comes and says, "You have had it, and sin is fresh and present in your life." When this happens to you, just remember that God intends to put down every enemy before your very eyes. You, as a witness, will watch Him subdue the enemy's dominion in your own nature. He will overthrow all power. You will watch God tear apart, thread-by-thread, dismantle, and bring to an end, everything that has ever discouraged you.

For years, I consistently faced the same lustful, moody, angry, hostile temptations, and the same uncontrolled lack of temperance in my life. The great lion after God's own heart (David) said, "Every day my enemy comes to eat up my flesh" (Ps. 27:2). Again and again, like David of old, I would fall into His arms – a thousand times, before I learned His arms were always there. The enemy says, "You are going to dash your foot against a stone." The Lord says, "I am going to hold you up." When you put on the helmet of salvation as a hope, hope begins to release an anointing in your life. When you face a situation that says: "It is a dead end, and now Pharaoh and his soldiers are coming behind; you have had it," right there and then, put on the helmet and say, "I put my hope in God." What a difference it makes in your life when you hope in God! If you want to see God work, let the enemy think he has you trapped and then make a confession in front of those who are accusing you of being the weakest Christian, who ever lived. Right in front of them say, "But I know Jesus lives, and I know He loves me and I know He is my shield; He is my defender. Besides that, He is my justifier; He is my redeemer. He is the One who took my sins in His own body; He set me free by Himself. He didn't ask for your vote on it; He said, I will do it. When He hung on the cross and said, 'It is finished,' it was finished, and it has been finished ever since."

Some of you need to get into your prayer closet and look at what is intimidating you until you say to the devil, "I don't know where I am going from here, but listen to me, I am shaking the dust off the soles of my feet. I am not going down; I am going forward. I cannot be defeated because I already have the victory. I don't have to fight to get the victory. Jesus fought the fight and got the victory, and He gave it to me in that robe of salvation." Put on the royal helmet, the hope of salvation. You can say to your husband, "Everything is going to be all right; I am going to live and not die." You can say to your wife, "Everything will be okay; we are going to make it. We are not going under; God is going to bring us through." Instead of saying to your children, "We are poor, and we are never going to make it; you were born into a poor family; don't ever expect anything better in your life," you can say, "We have hope in God. He is able to take the poor from the dunghill and set them on thrones with kings." This is the helmet we must wear. We are going forward in faith because the anointing is working in our lives. The anointing in Esther's life brought her out of the king's harem, made her queen, and loosed her neck from the noose that was made for her by Haman. He, himself hung there on the gallows made for Mordecai as Mordecai and his fellow Jews rode through the streets as princes and kings sitting on thrones built for others.

Chapter 10
The Carpenter's Anointing

Many ask the following questions:
1. What is my destiny?
2. Why am I here?
3. Where am I going?

These are very good questions; in fact, the best questions. What is God's will in your life? Why are you here? Why are you at your workplace? Why are you married to that particular person? Why are you single? Why have you come to the place you have come? How does the Spirit lead and pull everything together? The answer to all these questions and more is this: That you might let Christ's life be shown through your life. That is why God put His anointing in us. God's purpose for all believers is to let Christ's life shine through us, regardless of the setting or the circumstance. Jesus Christ lived the perfect, successful, triumphant, victorious life, which no one before Him ever did, and no one – of themselves – has done since that time. There is no perfection in the flesh or outside of Him. He has brought us to a new life.

"Now it came to pass, when Jesus had finished these parables, that He departed from there. When He had come to His own country, He taught them in their synagogues, so that they were astonished and said, "Where did this Man get this wisdom and these mighty works?" (Matt. 13:53-54)

155

ANOINTED TO ROAR

Where do you get Christ's wisdom? Where do you get Christ's works? Where do you get the Christ-life? These are the questions we are going to focus on in this chapter.

"Is this not the carpenter's son? Is not His mother called Mary? And His brothers James, Joses, Simon, and Judas? And His sisters, are they not all with us? Where then did this Man get all these things?" (Matt. 13:55-56)

How did this man (Jesus) get these things? How did He get this wisdom? How did He become 'The Lion, the King of beast's' whose roar carries such authority in the kingdom of God? How is it that when He shows up and roars that demons cry out? How is it that when He speaks a word, sickness leaves? How is it that the very wind and waves obey His voice? How can we get what He has? How can we become such a princely lion king and roar in such majesty, power and authority? The answer, in part, is that He got them through the anointing in the carpenter's house, and we can also get them in the carpenter's house, where a life is constructed that is able to hold the highest anointing.

As we continue on in this teaching on being Anointed to Roar and on how the anointing functioned in the lives of several men and women of God, we come to perhaps the most important of all – Joseph – the earthly father of Jesus. In considering why God chose Joseph to be the earthly father of Jesus, the type of man he was, his work, etc., we will find much that we can relate to. Joseph is one of the most unique characters in the Bible. He was considered the guardian of the Messiah. All believers, like Joseph, have been made guardians of the Messiah. When you become a Christian, Jesus was born into you, and you were born into Him. In one sense, He becomes your guardian, and in

156

another sense, He asks you to become the guardian of the Christ life. Being a Christian is more than just doing good, it is receiving a new life. What kind of person did God choose to put in charge as the overseer of the Messiah (Christ life)? He didn't choose a politician, a soldier, or a farmer; He chose a carpenter. Why would God choose a carpenter, and what can we learn from this? God chose a man who could look at a pile of wood and see something beautiful. He chose a man who could look at the clutter of leftover pieces and say, "Now I could form that into this; I could cut it here; I could put this together there; I could fasten it tight, and I could take some of the leftover pieces, and make them into trinkets of beauty, or into tools or instruments of craft and skill." A skilled carpenter can look at a piece of ground and say, "We can build right here, move this, move that, dig down so many inches, and find some old boards to use in laying the foundation." The first time I took notice of laying a foundation was when I hired a cement layer to expand my back patio around the full extent of the back area at our house. I was shocked at how they did it. The builders used dirty, ugly, knot-hole filled old boards and placed them around the borders of the foundation. They lined them up and set up a board here and a board there. I said, "What are you going to do with those ugly things?" They replied, "When we get all the cement laid in, we will pull down those boards; then we'll shape it, fashion it, and make it beautiful." They took something I would have thrown away and used it to lay a foundation.

Carpenters and Construction workers know how to lay a foundation, and upon it to build a wall, and upon the wall, to build the rafters, and upon the rafters, the roof. God chose a man who knew how to take things that were disorderly and disconnected – things with no beauty in them – pieces of rocks and boards piled here and there, and bring them together, and under divine order, to produce something beautiful and powerful. In relating that concept to the theme of this teaching, I am calling the way the anointing functioned in Joseph's life the Carpenter's Anointing. We can learn much about Joseph as we look at the product that came out of his carpenter's shop – Jesus, the Messiah, The Lamb and The Lion. Even though I spent most of my young life serving the Lord since I was sixteen, and even though I graduated from Bible school at the top of my class, I almost turned away from being a preacher. I told God that I could serve Him just as well being a businessman. (I had a high paying full time job as a businessman for many years while still working in full time ministry). Although I was being pulled in two different directions I still worked hard at being one of the very best in my field of marketing. However, Jesus didn't call me to be a businessman; He called me to be a preacher. I decided I could be a witness in the marketplace, as a gospel-preaching businessman, and share Jesus Christ from that platform. To be honest the real reason I thought about being a businessman was because number one, I was afraid that I could never be able to support my family financially on the salary of a full time pastor, and secondly, because the root of my fear and feelings of inadequacy. I couldn't make sense out of Christianity. I couldn't put scriptures together then as I can now. I didn't know why one thing meant something in one place, and something else in another. I couldn't understand why one minister would preach from a text and explain it one way, and then another preacher would come and preach from the same text and explain it in an entirely different way. I thought all full gospel ministers should be saying the exact same thing. I didn't know then that every Word of God has at least seven dimensions of revelation and knowledge – at least seven! The Bible says: "The words of the Lord are pure words: as silver tried in a furnace of earth, purified seven times" (Ps. 12:6). Because I couldn't comprehend deeper truths back then, I said, "I can never make sense of it all; I don't ever want to be accused of leading God's people astray or run the risk of teaching heresy." I started an in depth study of scriptures and Bible doctrine. I also gave myself to the study of the Greek and Hebrew, and I learned texts such as "Let the words of my mouth, and the meditation of my heart, be acceptable in thy sight, O Lord, my strength and my redeemer" (Ps. 19:14 KJV). Those words began to be written on the tablets of my heart. They were a pile of timber lying in my soul, so whenever the Holy Spirit needed a truth to build with He had a pile to draw from.

How does one scripture connect with another? God, in time, gave me a carpenter's mind that enabled me to bring truths together and fasten them in place. I could suddenly see the doorway, a hallway, and then a room. I could see various building blocks of God's Word fashion themselves into a place where I could live my spiritual life; a place where I could function and work; a place from where I could confidentially teach others. I was an apprentice being taught by the foreman of the scriptures, the Holy Spirit. As I learned more from my teacher and mentor, the Holy Spirit, I began to become more and more confident as a builder of truth. Wisdom, stature, and favor didn't just happen for Jesus. The Bible tells us that He grew up into those things. Luke 2:52 says, "And Jesus increased in wisdom and stature, and in favor with God and man." If you want to see the Christ life in your daily walk, it is necessary for you to experience a time of growth. Don't be in a big hurry to get through Bible school so you can get out and preach. You need to slow down and grow. Instead of looking for a public ministry, start looking for a place to grow so the Christ life will be manifested in your walk. However, more important than the place of growth is the process of growth. If you are unhappy where you are, stop trying to be happy there and concentrate only on letting the Christ life show forth.

1 Corinthians 3:9 KJV says, "For we are laborers together with God: ye are God's husbandry, ye are God's building." This is a dual allegory; we are both a field and a building. Hereby we learn that the growth comes by a preplanned design, and that gives the principle of planned development. The pattern of growth in human beings is in the genes. There is also a pattern in the growth and development of plants. For example, when you plant a grapevine, you don't get figs, you get grapes. God has created within each species of plant the power to reproduce itself generation after generation. This principle also applies to the Christ life within us. It will manifest God's likeness in us because it is created that way, but participation on our part is necessary for it to come together. You can't have a vine growing on an arbor unless you plant the vine by the arbor. That is where the two allegories come together. You have to build the house, build the arbor, attach the arbor to the house, and plant the vine by the arbor.

We are told in Psalms that a virtuous wife is like a vine on an arbor by a house (see Ps. 128:3), and we, the Body of Christ, are the Bride of Christ. So, at this point, the allegories run together, showing that participation and cooperation are required. We cannot just sit around and say, "There is no house here." We must say, "God, you see in my life and circumstances, adequate provisions to lay a foundation, put up walls, finish a building and have a house in which Jesus Christ can live out His full life in our generation, just like He did in the New Testament." That is what Christianity is all about.

THE CARPENTER'S ANOINTING

1 Corinthians 3:10 NIV says, "By the grace God has given me, I laid a foundation as an expert builder (KJV – "wise master builder") and someone else is building on it, but each one should be careful how he builds." How does a wise master builder build? Jude 1:20 NIV says, "But you, dear friends, build yourselves up in your most holy faith and pray in the Holy Spirit." The first question is: Do you want the Christ life manifested in your life? Do you think it can happen if you don't follow the same patterns the apostles followed? No way! The book of Jude says to pray in the Holy Spirit and build up yourself. Are you praying in the Holy Spirit regularly? Are you praying the mysteries of heaven for your own life in your Spiritual language (the gift of tongues), and in Spirit-anointed utterances in your own English language? If not, begin to do so immediately. If you don't have the Baptism of the Holy Spirit with the evidence of speaking with other tongues, God is ready and willing to grant you this blessing right here and now.

Most Christians—charismatics included— don't understand the true benefits of speaking in tongues, nor why this gift is so valuable. Here are 10 reasons to prove why we need this wonderful gift:

1. The manifestation that came with the gift of the Holy Spirit was speaking in tongues. It wasn't the wind, fire, noise or feeling of God's presence that was evidence of the gift being received, but a spirit language—believers began speaking languages of the Spirit they didn't understand. It was God's plan for the gift to function as a spirit language for His children (Acts 2:4; 11; 1 Cor. 14:2).
2. Jesus commanded us to receive the gift of the Holy Spirit. When Jesus commissioned the disciples to wait in

Jerusalem until they received the promise of the Father, He didn't say, "Do this if you feel led to do so, or if it fits in your doctrinal or denominational beliefs if you have the time, if you are so inclined, or if you feel comfortable about it." No! Jesus commanded them to wait until they received the gift of the Holy Spirit. Since Jesus put such importance on them receiving this gift, that's more than enough reason for every Christian to seek God until they receive it too (Acts 1:4; 5:32; John 14:16-17; Eph. 5:18).

3. The Scriptures exhort us to be filled with the Spirit and to pray in the new tongues of our spirit language. Our spirit language enables us to live in the Spirit, walk in the Spirit, be lead of the Spirit, have the fruit of the Spirit, manifest the gifts of the Spirit and go from glory to glory until we are transformed into His same image (Gal. 5:22-25; Rom. 8:14; 1 Cor. 12:7-11; Eph. 5:18; Acts 19:2; 2 Cor. 3:18).

4. A spirit language is the greatest gift the Holy Spirit can give a believer. Jesus is the greatest gift God could give for the redemption of the world, and the Holy Spirit is the greatest gift Jesus could give to His church. Of all the resources in heaven and the eternal universe, nothing is more valuable, beneficial or important for the Holy Spirit to give the individual child of God than her own spirit language (1 Cor. 12:31; 14:4).

5. Speaking in tongues enables us to have spirit-to-Spirit communication with God. Humans are spirit beings clothed with flesh-and-bone bodies. While man's sin deadened the spirit, Jesus brings the spirit back to life by imparting His everlasting life into us. The Holy Spirit gives us a spirit language so we can communicate directly with God (John 4:24; 1 Cor. 15:45; Gen. 2:7; Rom. 5:12; John 3:3-5, 16).

6. Praying in tongues builds and increases our faith. Faith is the medium of exchange for all heavenly things, just as money is the medium of exchange for all earthly things. A major way to increase our faith is to pray in the tongues of our spirit language (Rom. 12:6; Jude 1:20; Mark 9:23; Matt. 9:29).

7. Praying in tongues activates the fruit of the Spirit. It is vital and beneficial to have each of the spiritual attributes become active and mature in us. Praying in tongues helps us fulfill God's predestined purpose for us to be conformed to the image of His Son (Gal. 5:22-23; 2 Cor. 3:18; 1 Cor. 13:1-13; Rom. 8:29).

8. Praying in our spirit language is the main way we fulfill the scriptural admonition to "pray without ceasing." Christians can pray in tongues at any time. If we are in a place where it isn't convenient or wise to speak out loud in tongues, we can pray with our inner man without making an audible sound (Eph. 6:18; 1 Thess. 5:17; Matt. 26:41; Luke 18:1; 21:36; 1 Cor. 14:15).

9. The Holy Spirit directs our spirit language to pray in accordance with the will of God. Probably the only time we can be assured that we are praying 100% in the will of God is when we are praying in our spirit language. God always answers requests that are made in alignment with His will (Rom. 8:27; 1 John 5:14-15).

10. Praying in tongues quiets the mind. When Dr. Andrew Newberg (a neuroscientist), compared brain scans of Christians praying in tongues with Buddhist monks chanting and Catholic nuns praying, the study showed the frontal lobes—the brain's control center—went quiet in the brains of Christians speaking in tongues. This proves that speaking in tongues isn't a function of the natural brain but an operation of the spirit (1 Cor. 14:2; 14).

ANOINTED TO ROAR

Are you ready to receive the fullness the gift of tongues in your life? Just call out to Him and the sweet precious Holy Spirit baptism of fire will come upon you and begin to fill your mouth with tongues of fire! You don't need some well-known evangelist, pastor, or prophet to lay hands on you. You just need to call out to Jesus, and He will send to you the Holy Spirit, who will come upon you, envelop you, overshadow you and infill you! He will roar over your life with His power, blessing, favor, and Spiritual gifts.

Now, let's get back to the subject of *"building up"*. Many sons could have grown up in Mary and Joseph's house who did not learn to walk as Jesus walked – though they went through the same learning steps. They learned the same procedures, but they didn't apply them as Jesus did. That's the point we are getting at here. The "building up" is a process, and we, also, are required to do some of the building. "But let each one take heed how he builds on it. For no other foundation can be laid than that which is already laid, which is in Jesus Christ" (1 Cor. 3:10-11 NIV). This means that once you are born again, you don't have to worry about your foundations. You don't have to keep proving again and again that Jesus is Lord. However, you do have to start building faith, commitment, trust, hope, and obedience into your life. If you say you have faith, peace and power, but you do not obey, those things may take a turn in the wrong direction and not bear any fruit.

I Corinthians 3:12 KJV: "Now if anyone builds on this foundation with gold, with silver, with precious stones, wood, hay, and with stubble..." Straw and hay would be adequate material if you were making a basket. Straw is not a bad, inferior or negative material. So, something made of straw is not

164

necessarily bad or inferior. In fact, straw was the material used for making the baskets the disciples used to gather the leftovers when Jesus blessed and multiplied the bread and the fish. The material to be used for building depends on what is being built. In Jesus' time, they used straw to build thatched houses, and they used stones to build other houses. So, while the text above does not say any of these building materials are bad, it does say that certain ones can stand less testing than others. A house made from straw will go up in smoke and fire quicker than a house made from silver, but a silver house will melt in time with enough heat. A gold house will melt down in time; it will lose its form, but it will remain gold.

I Corinthians 3:13 KJV: "His work will be shown for what it is, because the day will bring it to light. It will be revealed with fire, and the fire will test the quality of each man's work." The point is that everyone is building a house – wood, hay, stone, straw, gold, silver – and each one's work will become manifest; "For the day will declare it because it will be revealed by fire – that is, a consuming force". We don't see fire physically coming in our churches, but we are all passing through the fire, whether we realize it or not. Jesus stood in the face of the fire that came upon Him. What was it about Him – what qualities did He have that enabled Him to do so? When the fire was gone, He was still standing there: Hebrews 13:8 says, "Jesus Christ is the same yesterday, today, and forever." True holiness causes you to remain unchanged in the face of burning fire, because the fire will reveal it, and test everyone's work as to what sort it is.

I Corinthians 3:14 KJV: "If anyone's work which he has built on endures, he receives a reward." Rewards come after testing. Five years ago, in our church, we had a congregation of about 120 solid, loyal, committed, servant, tithing people standing with us.

God showed me in 2009 like in the book of Zechariah that two-thirds of them would go through the fire, and one-third, the remnant, would stay on the outside praying and interceding for those on the inside, going through the fire. Before we got out of the fire, we dropped from 120 down to only 40 people. Due to the extreme impact of the economy and people shrinking back in their commitments and leaving, we had lost our beautiful 20k sq. ft. church facility that we were enjoying so much. We were forced to leave from there and move into a small broken down Church of God building located in Maryvale, Arizona; it was a blessing to have a place to fall back on, but we had trouble keeping people coming to services because it was located in a very unsafe and undesirable area of town. We only endured it for a brief 2 year period until we were invited to move into a small, but newer building and cohabitate with a new Messianic Congregation in the city of Peoria, Arizona. We felt like failures. There we were, we had come full circle from where we had initially begun our ministry 16 years prior, and with the same amount of people. We were where we first started in small humble beginnings. We were broken in spirit and broke financially, yet we were still determined to continue to build up the church and follow the leading of the Holy Spirit wherever he would lead. Then, one Sunday, seemingly from nowhere, new people started coming and joined the church. We said, "Where in the world are these people coming from?" They were loving, supportive, caring, and giving people who became involved in various ministries, in the church. They are helping us build, and the church is growing again. Since then, my wife, my family, and I, and those 40 people who stayed with us through it all, are being rewarded by God because we remained faithful and steady. We are now reaping the rewards because someone said, "I'm going to build on the foundation of Jesus Christ with right attitudes." Throughout the trials, burning, struggling, and fears, more of the Christ came out and less of the self.

I Corinthians 3:15 KJV: "And if anyone's work is burned, he will suffer loss, but he himself will be saved." We are not preaching destruction upon people or churches. We are preaching, rather, that there are some people, and some situations in homes and churches that can only be purged by fire for the salvation of that church, that home, or that individual. Whether we like it or not, we must be tested in order to experience the reality of God's power in our lives. The result is: Instead of going down with the forces of the fire; we come through the fire. We must check to see if we are building our lives on the foundation of Jesus Christ. Our goal as we focus on the "Carpenter's Anointing" is to understand what it means to be brought into the place of development and growth, the place where the carpenter puts His hand upon our lives. At the Carpenter's house, we not only get the construction and development of the temple of God, out of which the glory of the Christ-life is seen, but we see an end brought to the forces of adversity, hostility, and destruction that come against us. We rejoice in knowing that when the enemy rushes in, the Lord calls His carpenters, and they whittle him down to size. In the Carpenter's house, you learn to gather, assemble, and build things that may outlive you. In some of the great cities of America – and even more so in other parts of the world – most of the builders of those magnificent buildings are dead. The buildings remain, showing that man's creative capacity is greater than man's physical life, testifying that man's touch with God creates in us an eternal quality of life that goes on forever.

ANOINTED TO ROAR

Several Things Jesus Learned In The Carpenter's House

All the things Jesus learned in the carpenter's house are things we can incorporate and apply in our lives. He learned to say, "I must be about My Father's business." When Jesus was twelve years old, He and His parents and a host of other people from their city had traveled to Jerusalem for a time of celebration. But Jesus was so engrossed in talking with the teachers in the temple that He failed to depart with the group. When His parents came back and found Him in the temple, they asked Him, "What are you doing here? Didn't you know that your family had left?" Jesus answered, "Don't you know that I must be about my Father's business?" (see Luke 2:49). He had to learn to make the right choices. Throughout our lives, we are offered fleshly opportunities and spiritual opportunities. For example, tithing: Tithing does not seem like the best choice when considering what is best for the pocketbook. Yet tithing is the best choice when considering what is best for the spiritual man. Why? Because God said, "Bring all the tithes into the storehouse" (Mal. 3:10). A giving, careful person who wants to budget his income *and* honor God with the first-fruit of all his increase may at first say, "That's taking away from *my* table." He will also say, "But I have given to God, and he who gives to God will never be found in the poorhouse long." He may go to the poorhouse to find out how the poor suffer and how to witness to them, that if you believe God – even in your poverty – He will bring you out. If you are obedient and choose to tithe, you have chosen something that will render spiritual blessings in your life. After you have been tithing for a while, you may sometimes look at your finances and say, "I don't see any evidence that tithing has done us any good." That was the case with Jacob. Fourteen years later, he was still not prospering financially. He had prospered in his home and in his spirit – he had been brought to a place where he could believe God for miracles, and having faith to believe God for miracles is of more value than having a million dollars in a saving's account.

My wife's father, Jim Jackson, was a mechanic. His whole Jackson family were mechanics and 'fixers'; and good ones at that. Living with this master mechanic 'fixer', my wife also learned how to operate in the Jackson family 'gifting of fixing'. My wife, like her father, and his father before him could look at something that needs to be put together or required mending or repair, and they can have it completely put together or fixed in no time at all! I, however, am all thumbs when it comes to working with my hands. I always seem to have left over parts when building things or fixing things; especially at Christmas time with our kids new toys where "some assembly was required". My wife has learned over the years that whenever we see that sign on the box of new toys or furniture, immediately that project is assigned to her and not me. However, it wasn't always like this for her. It wasn't a hereditary gifting; it was learned. When my wife's father would say, "Phaedra, bring me that tool over there," She would bring him a tool, and he would say, "No, not that tool; I need the half-inch one." I'm sure that she would say, "I can't tell a half-inch tool from a three-quarter inch one." He would point it out to her, "That one over there." He could, by his trained eye, from across the garage, determine the difference in the size of the wrenches because he was practiced, experienced and selective. I am so glad that he took the time to pass on this training to her back then, as this has now become, many years later, a great blessing and stress reliever to me, her husband.

Learn to choose the right things: (1) the right attitudes and desires, (2) the right causes to champion, (3) the right things that are worth suffering for. It is because of wrong choices, selfishness, and things that are glittering in the eye at the moment that people all over the kingdom are suffering. Your choices must be based on these questions: "Would I give my life for it? Will this glorify Christ?" I learned what was right and what was wrong in the church where I grew up. My learning was based upon these questions: (1) Would Jesus do it? (2) Is this something that would come out of Him – the foundation? (3) Is this a window that would be found in a house that He would build? (4) Are these things He would say? (5) Is this the attitude He would have? I had to learn to make choices based on what Jesus would do. Jesus is the ultimate beauty and good of what the Bible teaches. All the law and commandments are fulfilled in the nature of Jesus. Jesus is the law manifested in human form in divine balance with the Carpenter's anointing. When you see a house that has been fitted and fashioned in such a way that everything fits together perfectly, you know, beyond any doubt, that it was built according to the master plan. You don't say, "Look at that door," or "Look at that roof." You say, "Look at that house. Look at the whole thing." When it is all put together correctly, no one aspect will stand out more than the others. If it does, it is not put together correctly. When it is put together correctly, it will be beautiful. One reason it is beautiful is the way the windows fit in. Another is the way the doors are fashioned to fit, and another is how they all blend so well with the roofing, etc. Nothing is over-done, and nothing is under-done; everything is done just right. Making right choices fashions a beautiful Christian life.

It Is Essential To Spend Time In Preparation
Jesus, from His birth to the age of thirty-three years, was in various stages of preparation. He learned patience in His early years. He learned even more patience when His parents brought Him home from the temple. He remained in subjection to them. How many more years of learning patience do we need to go

through? The answer is; as many as it takes! We sometimes say, "I can't take it." That is the problem; it has not 'taken'. But when it does take, you will sit at the Master Carpenter's feet and say, "Teach me Your ways. Show me how to understand what You are doing in my life." People can be so impatient. A promising minister once told me that if people could just recognize the great anointing upon his life, that his ministry would really take off. I said to him, "Brother, I do recognize your great anointing. Your anointing is one of the reasons I came to this service tonight, why I like to listen to your sermons and almost fall-out when you prophesy. I want an anointing like you have. I truly recognize your anointing, but it's obvious that God hasn't recognized something yet." It wasn't the anointing that God did not recognize. What the man did not recognize was the lack of discipline in some areas in his life, lack of death to self, and lack of knowledge as to how to apply the anointing.

You can also have an anointing and misuse it because you think, "If I have it; I should do something about it." Many preachers have told people: 'If you have it – use it'. If you don't use it – you'll lose it, but if you do use the anointing and don't learn patience, you may lose your anointing and your life. Some people without the wisdom, growth and stature, which give insight, balance and position above their enemies, have rushed in and have come back with stubs instead of fingers. They have literally been eaten up alive because they took on things too big for them, way too soon. Every local church, every family, and every Bible school is the Carpenter's house. Some people have said, "Well, by the time people get out of Bible school, all they know how to do is saw, saw, saw, and hammer, hammer, and hammer. They are always measuring things and looking at things, and they lose all their zeal and enthusiasm. Bible school can be a killer, but if you are one who can be killed by Bible school, you would have been killed by the ministry much sooner. You might as well discover early in your Christian life that few people are called to a pulpit ministry, but all are called to let the Christ-life shine between husband and wife, between parents and children and step-children. Jesus was a step-child to Joseph, who was charged with the responsibility of raising a child who could choose spiritual things, right things, and proper situations – a child who could be patient and wait on the Lord.

The Master Builder not only shows us the blueprints for the future, He also shows us the timing. People say, "I don't believe in that timing stuff anymore; it's just a big excuse to pull the wool over people's eyes." We should never disregard God's timing in any endeavor. Jesus had to wait on His Heavenly Father's timing before He started building the house that He was sent into this world to build. But when He did start to build it, He did it in God's timing and in God's ways. You say, "Yes, but look at what that other church did; they didn't have to wait. Why do we have to wait?" When Peter said to Jesus, "What about the things my other brothers are doing?" Jesus said, "It's none of your business. Your business is to follow Me." Out of the Carpenter's house came a man with such great wisdom, grace and balance, He could say, "Mind your business and keep your hand in God's hand; He will bring you to the place He wants you to be when He has made you ready to be there." A few years ago I heard a well-known preacher testify that he no longer needed to wear glasses because God had healed his vision. Then he stated how many years he had been seeking God for healing, and I was devastated because I had believed God to heal me of asthma for several years. I said to myself, "If a man of his faith and stature had to wait that long, how long do I have to wait to be healed?" But under the Carpenter's anointing, I turned my doubt into faith, and chose not to carry that yoke and burden, but to let the anointing say, "If he could wait it out and walk it out, then so can I." Faith, patience, persistence and the willingness to let God teach us, lead us, and guide us, will enable us to walk the same way Jesus walked. Jesus fasted forty days and forty nights. That was a time of testing and temptation for Him. Others would have cracked and crumbled under that test, but He didn't. What did He learn in the Carpenter's shop that kept Him from cracking and crumbling? What did He learn that kept Him from yielding to the temptation? He learned that He must base His faith on the Word and not on His circumstances or feelings, or who He was in Himself, but on who He was in God. In the unrelenting temptation, He was still able to say, "But it is written."

When temptation comes our way, we must stand in the Word. When temptation or sickness threatens me, I find myself, more and more, taking the sword of the Spirit, the Word of God, and saying, "But God says…" As I stand in what God says, the playing field is leveled, and the enemy's awesome threats are reduced. More and more I understand God's favor toward me, and I find myself growing in stature in the presence of my enemy. God gifted Jesus with everything good, righteous, and wonderful. Jesus took all the things He was gifted with, along with all the things He had developed, and committed them totally to this one thing: "I will build My church and the gates of hell will not prevail against it." The Carpenter's anointing that was in Joseph's life, the overseer of the Christ-life, was finally focused toward building the church. Instead of sitting around and saying, "When is God ever going to use me?" get out of the Carpenter's shop and start moving out in the Christ-life ministry, witnessing, sharing, and testifying. We are an anointed, gifted people, and if we let the light we have shine at whatever level we are on, we will see something beautiful come out of our lives.

Chapter 11
The Anti-Anointing

Is There An Anti-Anointing?

Is there such a thing as an anti-anointing? Is there an anointing from the wicked one that empowers people to fight against the Holy Anointing? Jesus Christ of Nazareth is more than just an ordinary man called Jesus. Many were called Jesus. In the book of Exodus, Joshua means Jesus. In Zechariah, the name of one of the high priests was Joshua (Jesus). But the Jesus we preach is Jesus the Christ, the Messiah, the Son of the Living God. The word *Christ* means the "anointed one". Satan always has a counterfeit to everything good and holy that comes from God. There is in this world an anti-anointing. There is a dark energizing unction that opposes the anointing. What else could have been happening during times of insurrection and rebellion against divinely appointed leadership in the Word of God and throughout man's history?

Absalom was one of David's sons, growing up in the house of the anointed of the Lord. Psalm 89 is devoted to describing the anointing of David and the anointing upon his household that would never cease. There would always be an anointed one upon the throne of David. What else could have happened to David's favored son Absalom, the heir to the throne, the heir to the anointing, that he should be driven to overthrow his father David? What else could have caused Korah to rise up, resist, and rebel against the leadership of Moses and Aaron? What else

175

could have caused Cain to rise up in bitter anger against Abel's better offering to God?

To help you better understand this point, let me put this in a threefold setting:

1. The church
2. The home
3. The individual

When you serve God, walk in righteousness, and walk in the Spirit, God promises to bless both your physical and spiritual being. God promises to bless everything you put your hand to do. God promises that the anointing that flows out will bless you, heal you, prosper you, and teach you. Isaiah says the anointing breaks the yoke. Everything that binds you in the flesh, He will break. Yet, throughout Christendom today, people fight the message of obedience; they resist the message of holiness. People are ready to kill the prophets and pastors who call all people to repentance and to walk closer with God. They say, "That is not grace teaching that is legalism," they say, "That is Old Testament; That is bringing people under the law." But the Bible is clear that we are not without law to Christ. We are not under the Law of Moses but now we are under (or subject to) the law of Christ. We do not have the shadow any longer; we have the real Christ, and the real Christ is with us to bring us into obedience – not just in deed and word, but in every thought being brought into captivity to Him. This pertains to our personal life, our family life, and our church life.

THE ANTI-ANOINTING

The New Hyper-Grace Gospel vs. The Confess And Repent Gospel

I believe that the new hyper-grace message being preached in today's churches of America is a modern day example of an anti-anointing working against the true anointing in the earth. What do hyper-grace preachers and ministries focus on? I find it easy to identify what they both focus on and what they ignore. So let's begin by looking at what hyper-grace folks focus on (I do acknowledge not all of it is wrong).

1. Salvation by Grace Through Faith.
   It seems some hyper-grace teachers want to protect the teaching of salvation by grace through faith (see Eph. 2:8-9). They honestly believe that adding repentance to this adds works to it and destroys salvation by grace through faith.

2. Works Obtain Righteousness.
   Hyper-grace teachers want us to avoid believing that our works obtain righteousness. They are correct of course in this regard. Our salvation is based on Jesus Christ and His work on the cross and not our works (see Titus 3:5-7). Jesus said that the work of God is to believe in the One that He has sent (see John 6:29). Our works writes Isaiah in Isaiah 64:6, "...are but filthy garments in His holy presence". This is not to demean works but to simply put down the notion of us obtaining God's perfect righteousness by our works (see Rom. 4:5).

3. Guilt Factors in Discipleship.
   We do not serve God out of guilt. We serve Him out of love. Some hyper-grace teachers want us to realize that

we can serve God out of love and not out of guilt. We don't pray, fast, read our Bibles, worship, enjoy fellowship with other disciples, etc. out of guilt but out of love. This, like above, is a good point.

4. Seeks To Avoid Making the Christian Life All About Us.
   The Christian life writes one hyper-grace teacher, is about Jesus. Amen! On this point, we can agree. The Christian life is all about Jesus (see Col. 3:1-4). Our lives are to be marked by a passion for Jesus and what He has done and not our works, our desires, our passions, our goals, etc. We are to focus on Jesus completely.

Now let us turn to the many errors of the hyper-grace teachers and what they often leave out:

1. Hyper-Grace Ignores Human Responsibility.
   Like the hyper-Calvinists, hyper-grace teachers avoid the clear call in the Bible to our response to the gospel and to the Lordship of Christ. True faith is never a dead faith (see James 2:14-26). True faith in Christ obeys Jesus as Lord (see Matt. 7:21-27; Luke 6:46-49; 1 John 2:3-6). Hyper-grace teachers avoid any call in the Bible to seek God, to obey God, to follow Christ, and to walk in the Spirit (see Gal. 5:16-17). I even found one hyper-grace teacher attacking preaching in the open air. He mocked this and quoted from Isaiah 42:2 "He will not cry out, nor raise His voice, nor cause His voice to be heard in the street" as proof that we should not preach in the open air.

2. Hyper-Grace Ignores Holiness Passages.
   There are so many holiness passages. We are to be pure in heart (see Matt. 5:8). We are to be perfect as our Father in

heaven is perfect (see Matt. 5:48). We are to consider ourselves dead to sin and alive to God in Christ Jesus (see Rom. 6:11). We are to complete holiness out of a healthy fear for God (see 2 Cor. 6:14-7:1). We are to examine ourselves (see 2 Cor. 12:21-13:5). We are to be blameless (see Phil. 2:15). We are to pursue holiness (see Heb. 12:14) and to be holy as God is holy (see 1 Peter 1:15-16). We are to forsake sin (see 1 John 3:4-10). Hyper-grace teachers avoid holiness passages altogether.

3. Hyper-Grace Ignores the Fact that 'We Cannot Worship God and Serve Satan'.
   1 Corinthians 10:21 says that we cannot drink both the cup of Christ and the cup of demons, as well. In context (see 1 Cor. 9:24-10:21), we cannot serve both God and Satan. To serve Satan ends in death (see James 1:12-15; 5:19-20). We cannot both walk in the Spirit and in the flesh at the same time (see Gal. 5:16-17). We cannot both love Christ and hate Him at the same time. We can, however, claim facts about Christ, but not truly know Him. Even the demons know God. "Even the demons believe—and tremble!" (James 2:19).

4. Hyper-Grace Views Any Discipline as Legalism.
   By discipline I mean the disciplines of prayer, worship, fasting, evangelism, and Bible study. If you say that a Christian should do these things, some hyper-grace teachers will cry, "legalism" and run for the hills. While none of these disciplines save us, they are proofs of our salvation (see Eph. 2:10). Jesus said we would pray (see Matt. 6:5) and fast (see Matt. 5:16). Jesus said that we would do good works for His glory (see Matt. 5:13-16; John 14:12). Jesus said that His followers would remain

in His Word (see John 8:31-32) which is able to save our souls (see James 1:21). While we cannot obtain God's righteousness by our disciplines, our disciplines flow from our relationship and divine justification.

5. Hyper-Grace Ignores Sanctification.
    I have yet to hear a hyper-grace teacher teach on 1 Thessalonians 4:3 and the need for sanctification. Most hyper-grace teachers believe at the moment a person is saved (just once and only once is sufficient no matter how the person lives their lives), that person is now glorified in the eyes of God. They see our glorification as already done, so that progressive sanctification is completely ignored. They see no need to stress holiness, obedience to Christ as Lord, etc. since a 'once saved' person is forever saved and has already been glorified before God because of Christ.

6. Hyper-Grace Despises Repentance.
    Most hyper-grace teachers despise repentance. They see it as a form of works-righteousness, of legalism, and bondage. They see repentance as completely negative instead of seeing it as a positive (see 2 Cor. 7:10; 2 Peter 3:9).

7. Hyper-Grace Teachers Read the Bible With Dispensational Scissors.
    Many hyper-grace teachers will usually camp in the Gospel of John and the Epistles (except not the books of Hebrews or James) but they avoid the other three Gospels and view them as 'under the law'. For instance, one hyper-grace teacher commented on his internet blog, "The gospel of John never uses repentance so why should we?" The answer is of course because the Bible uses it. 2

Timothy 3:16-17 says that ALL Scripture is "inspired" and "God breathed" and Paul was referring to the O.T. Further, Paul says in 2 Timothy 3:16, about the O.T. mind you, that it is profitable for teaching, for reproof, for correction, and for training in righteousness. If this is true of the O.T., it is true of Matthew, Mark, Luke, Hebrews, and James. To divide the Scriptures up like this has no warrant other than theological bias.

8. Hyper-Grace Ignores the Book of Acts.
   The book of Acts is full of salvation and repentance and even necessary perseverance (see Acts 2:38; 3:19; 4:12; 11:18; 14:22-23; 16:30-34; 17:30-31; 26:20). Hyper-grace teachers will sometimes use Acts 15 to preach against 'legalism' as they see it, or sometimes will appeal to Acts 16:31 for salvation but will ignore the calls to repentance.

9. Hyper-Grace Provides Comfort For the Sinning.
   The Bible offers no assurance to the person who lives in consistent sin. None! 1 John 3:4-10 is clear: "Whoever commits sin also commits lawlessness, and sin is lawlessness. And you know that He was manifested to take away our sins, and in Him there is no sin. Whoever abides in Him does not sin. Whoever sins has neither seen Him nor known Him. Little children, let no one deceive you. He who practices righteousness is righteous, just as He is righteous. He who sins is of the devil for the devil has sinned from the beginning. For this purpose the Son of God was manifested, that He might destroy the works of the devil. Whoever has been born of God does not sin, for His seed remains in him, and he cannot sin, because he has been born of God. In this, the children of God and

the children of the devil are manifest: Whoever does not practice righteousness is not of God, nor is he who does not love his brother."

In fact, the same John the Beloved who wrote the Gospel of John also wrote this in 1 John 2:1-6: "My little children, these things I write to you, so that you may not sin. And if anyone sins, we have an Advocate with the Father, Jesus Christ the righteous. And He Himself is the propitiation for our sins, and not for ours only but also for the whole world. Now by this we know that we know Him, if we keep His commandments. He who says, "I know Him," and does not keep His commandments, is a liar, and the truth is not in him. But whoever keeps His word, truly the love of God is perfected in him. By this, we know that we are in Him. He who says he abides in Him ought himself also to walk just as He walked."

I remind you that the same John the Beloved also wrote in Revelation 21:7-8: "He who overcomes shall inherit all things, and I will be his God and he shall be My son. But the cowardly, unbelieving, abominable, murderers, sexually immoral, sorcerers, idolaters, and all liars shall have their part in the lake which burns with fire and brimstone, which is the second death."

I end this particular discussion by also quoting from the same John the Beloved and the words from our Lord in John 8:4-11: "They said to Him, "Teacher, this woman was caught in adultery, in the very act. Now Moses, in the law, commanded us that such should be stoned. But what do You say?" This they said, testing Him, that they might have something of which to accuse Him. But Jesus stooped down and wrote on the ground with His finger, as though He did not hear. So when they continued asking Him, He raised Himself up and said to them, "He who is without sin among you, let him throw a stone at her first." And again He stooped down and wrote on the ground. Then those who heard it, being convicted by their conscience, went out one by one, beginning with the oldest even to the last. And Jesus was left alone, and the woman standing in the midst. When Jesus had raised Himself up and saw no one but the woman, He said to her, "Woman, where are those accusers of yours? Has no one condemned you?" She said, "No one, Lord." And Jesus said to her, "Neither do I condemn you; go and sin no more."

Throughout our earthly lives, Jesus and His Spirit intercede for us (see Rom. 8:26; 8:34; Heb. 7:25; 1 John 2:1). This suggests that even though forgiveness has been utterly accomplished on the cross, it must still be applied to our lives. Forgiveness is applied, not only through intercession but also through confession of our sins. In order to be forgiven, confession is mandatory. If we claim to be without sin, we deceive ourselves and the truth is not in us. If we confess our sins, He is faithful and just and will forgive us our sins and purify us from all unrighteousness (see 1 John 1:8-9).

No one who is born of God will continue to sin, because God's seed remains in them; they cannot go on sinning because they have been born of God (see 1 John 3:9; 3:3; 5:18). The hyper-grace folks understand the heavenly, eternal perspective. However, they have ignored the earthly, material perspective or process. As a result, they ignore Jesus' warning against the wages of sin. The scripture is very clear in Romans 6:23 where the Apostle Paul eloquently reminds us that "the wages of sin is death." They ignore John's assertion that God's children will not continue in the practice of sin and the absolute necessity to confess our sins to receive forgiveness and cleansing. Consequently, the hyper-grace people preach a highly defective message. It is an anti-anointing that fights against the true Lion anointing of divine authority. Divine authority punishes wrongdoers and wrongdoing and rewards the righteous and righteousness.

Anti-Anointing Is The Cause of Division In The Church

Have you ever wondered why there are so many church splits today? Although it seems as if they are becoming more and more frequent in the local churches of America, this is not a new phenomenon, they have been going on from the very first age of the church. Paul and Barnabas had a big split. Peter and Paul fought face to face. What makes people feel driven to overthrow leadership, and to overthrow their family? The number one complaint from teenagers is that their parents don't love them. What gets a hold of young people and makes them believe their parents don't love them? Those parents picked up their babies the minute they were born and loved them, cared for them, changed their messy diapers, and walked the floor with them when they cried at night. They did everything for them, and then, all of a sudden, the children say, "My parents don't love me." How could children be so blind? How could Christian children get into an anti-parent attitude that may last for years as they try to destroy the leadership of the parents, their marriages, even over their very lives? How many news headlines do we see of some young teenage, son or daughter, being taken to prison for plotting and carrying out a vicious attack or murder against their parents? There has to be a deceptive force that makes people feel so right about such a wrong. "Woe to those who call evil good, and good evil; Who put darkness for light, and light for darkness; Who put bitter for sweet, and sweet for bitter! Woe to those who are wise in their own eyes, and prudent in their own sight!" (Isa. 5:20-21)

THE ANTI-ANOINTING

Absalom had to feel good about what he was doing to his father, David. Every day he went down and stood at the gates to the city and told the people, "Come over here. If I were king, I wouldn't treat you the way my father treats you. When I become king things will be different." This same anti-spirit is extremely prevalent in the churches of America today. It appears wise and prudent in their own eyes, but it is a self-anti-appointing anointing. People say, "If I were the Pastor, things would be much different." "If I were running this company, things would be much different." The carnal nature rises up, and it can give you a wonderful feeling, or sensation. It says, "If you will follow me... And quit going to church all the time, I will make you happy. Start drinking; start doing drugs, start having sex. Your parents are against it because they don't want you to have any fun. The reason that old preacher gets up there, and talks against social drinking is because he is an old grouch and needs to get with the times. He should probably have a good stiff drink; he would probably feel better. He is just a holy-roller and doesn't want you to have any fun! Come on there is nothing wrong with a little weed now and then, or a little snort up the nose."

All the illustrations above are associated with feelings. In many prophetic, Spirit-filled church circles, much of the focus is on feelings. This makes it so easy for a counterfeit feeling to lead you in an anti-scriptural endeavor or activity. When one is grounded in the Scriptures and the foundational doctrines of the Bible, those 'feelings' can be tested. Better yet, we do not seek to be lead by feelings, but by faith. If we equate God's anointing and leadership with feelings, we leave ourselves open to deception, for feelings are 'flesh,' and 'flesh' is so easily deceived. What else but an anti-anointing could have driven Miriam and Aaron to say, "We are prophets just as much as you, Moses. Who do you think you are?" Moses was God's appointed

185

servant, and through the revelation God had given to him, four hundred years of bondage and darkness had been broken. The question was not, "Could Miriam and Aaron hear God?" The fact is, God wants us all to hear Him; God created us to hear Him. I hear things in every service I am in. I hear things no matter who is in the pulpit preaching, but that does not mean that I have to come against the person who is in the pulpit and say, "The things I am hearing are much better than the things you are hearing." When I was newly saved as a teenager, I believed that I heard that I was to do special things for the Lord and needed to be available and free to do them, but that didn't give me the right to try and overthrow my parents authority and direction over my life. If they said "Yes son, you may have the freedom to go here or there for the Lord, I release you to go." Then I was properly released to go do them under the right anointing, but if they said to me, "No son, you are going to stay home and help us with all the chores around the house today." I wouldn't say to them, "I can't do that! I am anointed to do very special things for the Lord. Don't you know that I need to be, like Jesus needed to be, about my Father's business?" No, I needed to yield, surrender, and submit myself under my parents established leadership anointing over my life, or my father's spanking anointing would quickly come upon my backside and anoint my fanny! Any opposite response to established set authority is called rebellion. The Bible calls rebellion a wicked anti-anointing. According the scriptures, rebellion is referred to as witchcraft! In I Samuel 15:23 it says that rebellion "is as" the same exact as witchcraft. God absolutely despises both stubbornness and witchcraft, they are an abomination. "For rebellion is as the sin of witchcraft, and stubbornness is as iniquity and idolatry." (I Sam. 15:23)

"When you come into the land which the Lord your God is giving you, you shall not learn to follow the abominations of those nations. There shall not be found among you anyone who makes his son or his daughter pass through the fire, or one who practices witchcraft, or a soothsayer, or one who interprets omens, or a sorcerer, or one who conjures spells, or a medium, or a spiritist, or one who calls up the dead. For all who do these things are an abomination to the Lord, and because of these abominations the Lord your God drives them out from before you." (Deut. 18:9-12)

In the Word, God calls our rebellion the same as witchcraft. This truth is revealed in I Samuel 15, when Samuel was counseling Saul about why the Lord rejected him from being king over Israel. So Samuel said: "Has the Lord as great delight in burnt offerings and sacrifices, as in obeying the voice of the Lord? Behold, to obey is better than sacrifice, and to heed than the fat of rams. For rebellion is as the sin of witchcraft, and stubbornness is as iniquity and idolatry. Because you have rejected the word of the Lord, He also has rejected you from being king." Then Saul said to Samuel, "I have sinned, for I have transgressed the commandment of the Lord and your words, because I feared the people and obeyed their voice. Now, therefore, please pardon my sin, and return with me, that I may worship the Lord." But Samuel said to Saul, "I will not return with you, for you have rejected the word of the Lord, and the Lord has rejected you from being king over Israel." (I Sam. 15:22-26)

What this sad story reveals is that any time we turn from the one true God and try to make something happen through our own methods, we are, in a sense, involved in a type of witchcraft. When Adam and Eve were thrown out of Eden, they landed on all their 'ifs, ands, and buts.' We think, even today, that we have many good reasons for holding our heads high, proud of our accomplishments. In ignorance, we think that we should follow the world's commands to "make it on our own." This is rebellion. Why not recognize our inabilities? Why not be aware that, of ourselves, we can do nothing? Do we really want to spend time trying to convince God that we know what's best for us? In truth, God gave us our minds and hearts but by our free will, we chose to make choices contrary to our highest good. That happened first THEN we were barred from paradise. Now we live in a world where it is the norm to try and make it on our own, but do we really have the knowledge, the insight, the awareness that God has? In other words, we think we have the smarts to be in control of our lives, but do we? The human race didn't start out having to make it on its own. Our first ancestors lived in paradise, and pretty much everything was taken care of for them. Then when Satan stirred up rebellion in their hearts, God decreed that their sentence, as they were cast from Eden, was that "man should live by the sweat of his brow." This has been the way we've taken care of ourselves since that fateful time.

Now, as we continue to rebel, we strive to make our work easier with fewer working hours, giving us more and more leisure time, and what do we do with our leisure time? We have a wonderful array of entertainment systems with surround sound and wide TV screens that make everything look so real, it is quite magical. It is a magical kingdom we have dreamt for ourselves. "Almost like Heaven", we say to ourselves, and on these wide screens, almost as if we haven't had enough, we watch re-enactments of the very lives we lead. We take out the awkward parts and rearrange the events slightly, so that, dramatically, it gives a better punch, but who are we fooling? Only ourselves. Let's step back from this and ask God what He would prefer we spend our time doing. Really all we are watching are re-runs, viewing endless loops of the world and its sadness and its joys, its weak attempts to sculpt a meaning out of itself, but it will forever remain the fruit of the knowledge of good and evil. The world cannot make a paradise that can ever satisfy us truly. Yes, temporarily, it can squeeze a smile from us but our true joy and our true contentment can only come from God through Christ Jesus. Let's not fool ourselves any longer as we take paths that lead through the gaudy fake glitter the world offers. Let's set our minds and hearts toward God's Kingdom within. After all, technology has advanced so much; we DO have leisure time that we could use for more prayer time, more time for getting to know Jesus. We don't want to do this because we are rebels. When we make a space for prayer time in our day-timers, we may find, even as we are starting to kneel down, that there is something else we need to do. The proper use of our rebellious nature is when we choose to rebel against our rebellion. The reward of finding God within will be far more entertaining than anything the world could offer us.

Have you noticed that the pleasures of the world always turn sour? We so easily become enslaved to earning more money to buy more gadgets and toys. Sometimes having more leisure time actually causes our lives to become faster paced and more stressed. In addition, because of our carnal nature, we tend to misuse our leisure time on frivolous entertainment. We become couch potatoes, allowing every vice of humanity to enter our homes and our minds. Lust of every kind- greed, porn, and mammon in general comes pouring in and we who have forgotten where the on/off switch is, allow it to pollute us and make us feel ashamed. The entertainment industry cannot really be blamed because it is WE who beg for more. Its wheels will come to a grinding halt when we quit holding it upside down, trying to shake its cookies out of its cookie jar. It is only natural that it will stop at nothing to try and satisfy what appears as our endless desire for more and more filth to help us forget the reality around us. Is it the reality around us that makes us so sad, we feel we must escape it in some way? What did Jesus say about judging by appearances? He said not to do it. Instead, we do, thinking we are trapped in circumstances, bogged down in shame, and unable to withstand the onslaught of Satan in our lives. Our Lord and Savior, Jesus Christ, stands at the door, though, knocking. We must open the door to our hearts and let Him in. He will show us true rest and usher us out of our frantic worlds with its cold hands of death around our throats, just about to squeeze the life out of us. Jesus is the way out of this pathetic life that can hardly be called life at all. Jesus is the only true way out.

Yes, we tend to use our leisure time to seek thrills of either a physical or mental nature and this, then, consumes our time, as well as any thought of fellowship with God. I'm not saying we should resort to Spartan withdrawal from all that technology and entertainment has to offer. I am, however, saying we should guard our minds carefully and ask for the Lord's help more often because He, through us, will utilize all things for the glory of God. Ultimately, it is God we are trying to fill our lives with. We've just been lead astray by our bewitching rebellion; that is all. We prodigal sons will be welcomed back into the true warmth and comfort of our Father's arms. We were lost, but now we're found. So, we see that rebellion is an anti-anointing that says "I don't need to submit to an authority or direction. I am free to come, go, do, and serve my own will; and every whim and fleshly desire."

The problem we have had in Spirit-filled church circles is that there has been too much functioning in the anti-anointing of the flesh. It is easy to get sucked into this anti-anointing when you become rebellious against divine order. When you become discontented and unhappy, not pleased with your lifestyle, your marriage, your church, your lot in life, you become agitated. I have been in the pulpit ministry for 33 years. People who have been saved five and ten years want to come along and say to me, "We know this and we know that; who do you think you are?" It isn't even reasonable that a five year-old Christian could know what a person knows who has been following Christ for thirty three years. Let's be logical. Sometimes we need to sit down, shut up, and use our God given common sense and reasoning skills and think! I'm telling you; sometimes we need a check-up – from the neck up! Let's check up on ourselves and see who has been dumping garbage into our ears, and see how many of those tingling little sensations that have been getting a hold of us and making us feel good about how awesome we are is actually an anti-anointing of rebellion. The devil would like to give you an unction to agree with those who are involved in church splits, family splits, or with other things that cause division, and he would like to do so without you ever hearing the other part of the story and without considering what the Bible says. For example, the Bible is against divorce except for the cause of sexual impurity – period. I realize that when we attempt to negotiate people's problems, and help them deal with the stress they live under and the difficulties they are in we must consider their hurts, weaknesses, and inability to work things out. We do need to give consent to that, but, I also say, how can a person look straight at the Bible that says: "You shall not do such and such, and say', "But the Holy Spirit told me it was alright and I should do it?" There is something not right here that we need to consider.

In Numbers 23 what caused Balaam, after God said, "Don't go and prophesy against Israel," to go and do it anyway? When God pronounced a blessing instead of a curse, the king said, "You didn't do it good enough. I will pay you money if you will go back and do it again." Balaam said, "God said I can't do it." But later he said, "I will do it." Finally, the donkey said, "What are you doing? (I'm paraphrasing here). Don't you see the angel, the anointed one, standing in the way? You are coming against the very anointed purposes of God in this situation." What else could this be but an anti-anointing force and power that is able to seduce us?

People who are rebelling against anointed leadership will react in many ways. They could go from just sitting with arms folded and say, "I am not listening to a thing he says," to going around the church and finding people and pulling on them and complaining about the leadership. If we have ears to hear what the Spirit is saying, we would just simply refuse to listen to those people. We would say, "I am going to keep my nose in the Bible and continue to support my leadership". You will have to do what you have to do with your attitude. The Word says to "endeavor to keep the unity of the Spirit in the bond of peace." The problems some people are having will be resolved by getting back into the Word, and getting back into fasting and praying, and thoroughly cleansing our hearts before the Lord.

The Battle Between The Flesh and The Spirit

We are in a battle between the flesh and the Spirit. We can walk in the flesh, and if we do, we will yield our members as instruments to the devil, and we will be obedient servants to evil and demonic forces. Or we can walk in the Spirit and yield our members as instruments unto righteousness, and our lives will be in the service of the Holy Spirit. The anointing breaks the yoke, and the yoke is the flesh. The anointing destroys the burden, and the burden is sin. All morals are yoked in a body of flesh and burdened with sin. No matter what psychology says, the root of the problem is sin. No matter how many peoples' temperament adjustments come through counseling and psychology – which I recognize does occur – the real problem is still sin. Without the power of the blood, the power of the Word, and the power of the Spirit, even the most well-adjusted, transformed individual is still only a well-adjusted sinner. A person walking in the flesh can smile and even get excited and dance around in a Jericho march before the Lord in a church service. I have watched people during services, they dance with us and smile with us, but when I preach the Word, they can't sit and listen to the Word, and they walk out. Why? Because the Word of God conveys the anointing, and whatever is touched by the Living Word is anointed.

The anointing is the moving of the Spirit. The moving of the Holy Spirit comes in many ways. One of those ways is conviction. Most people in Charismatic churches can't stand any conviction at all. The moment they start getting a little convicted, they become subject to deception because they resist conviction and say, "There isn't anything wrong with me; I'm covered by grace." But, when grace is used as a cloak to cover sin and flesh, it is perverted and twisted, and it will lead to destruction. There is a deceptive, demonic power that creeps into people's thinking which causes them to think, "If I feel at peace; it's okay." Feeling peace is no criteria to having the peace of God, that keeps you in obedience to the Word. People can do exactly the opposite of what God's Word says, and still declare, "But I had peace about it." Just because a person has peace about something doesn't make it right. God's peace is a gift; any other kind of peace is a deception. Many people have thought they were following God when they were actually following their own feeling of peace, even while practicing sin. Take a look at Absalom. One of the elements that allowed him to be driven to overthrow the spiritual rule in his life, and to feel good about doing that which was wrong, was the element of discontent. Satan will do everything he can possibly do to get us in a state of discontentment. Our aim is to be in a state of godliness with contentment.

Psychologists are not interested in leading people into a state of contentment according to Bible rules. They are only interested in applying a principle that will lift the pressure and bring their patients out from under psychosomatic sickness, or twisted temperament, or anxiousness, etc. No matter what theory or method they use, if it helps people feel better, they believe it works, and they get paid for that. God is not just interested in making us feel better; He is interested in us learning to be content in whatever state we are in. "Now godliness with contentment is great gain." (I Tim. 6:6)

It wasn't until just a few years ago, that I could peacefully delegate responsibility in my church and Bible college ministries. I felt as if I had to do everything myself. Not being able to delegate responsibility is a terrible burden. When there are great responsibilities, we must learn to give some of them to other people, and then stay out of their way and let them work everything out. We must let things develop as God would have them develop. We can get into situations where we try to play God – in our lives, in the church, and in the home. Some husbands develop a god-mentality. They swell up, square their shoulders and say, "You will do what I tell you to do because the Bible says you are to submit to me!" Using the Word of God in that manner leads to sin and violence, and it is equally sinful and vile for a wife to be in verbal anarchy to her husband. The Bible says we are to submit ourselves to one another in the fear of God, wives to husbands, and husbands to wives. We must recognize the deceiving work of unrighteousness that keeps us hiding behind wrong.

As soon as a person is born again, he or she is filled with a drive to be like Jesus, and immediately starts trying to know what is right and wrong and to do what is right as much as possible. Most of us, within six months after we have been born again, fail so many times when we try to live according to our own list of rights and wrongs, that by the time the preacher comes and starts reading from the Book, "Thou shall not commit adultery, thou shall not steal, thou shall not lie...," we are overwhelmed with the great battle between the flesh and the Spirit. The works of the flesh are manifested in lying, hating, murder, greed, idolatry, sowing contention and division, backbiting and many attitudes and manners of conduct. Jesus is manifested in our flesh to destroy these works. When we hear these things, what must we do? We must be washed, cleansed, transformed, renewed, and we must absolutely stop practicing sin and start practicing being what God created us to be. God says not to walk after anything of the flesh. We must be careful lest after trying hard to defeat the flesh from being fleshly, we get to the point where we start believing the seducing spirits that tell us that it doesn't matter, and we don't have to put to death our members, which are upon the earth. This is anti-Christ (anti-anointing). The truth is that the anointing in your life will be weakened through the practice of sin. This teaching is not about who is going to make it to Heaven. It is not an attack on people for their sin-life. It is a teaching to expose you to the fact that Jesus came into your life, into your spirit, into your soul, and into your body. "Do you not know that your body is the temple of the Holy Spirit? Do you not know that when you commit fornication you have joined the body of God to the harlot?" I am quoting from the scriptures. (1 Cor. 6:19-20) "This kind of stuff ought not be."

There are grievous wolves that are coming in among the people of God today and telling us that practicing sin is all right because we are under grace and not under law. They tell us that practicing sin is all right because God understands our weaknesses. They say that God understands the weaknesses of fathers who are molesting their own daughters. A man mentioned in 1 Corinthians 5 was having sex with his father's wife. It was for that reason he was put out of the church. Yet, in the church today, people will listen to these evil spirits that come along and say, "But God understands." Others will say, "Oh, that preacher is too hard on you." We must acknowledge that we cannot live the life we should without God's help, and every day we must say, "I am going to yield my body a living sacrifice." Yielding our members a living sacrifice means that we give up to Christ all the areas of our lives, which are sinful, carnal, ungodly, and unkind, and say, "Self is wrong and Christ is right. The Christ in me is greater than the self-life in my carnal nature. Christ has come to conquer these motions of sin that are in my members". We must look at what the Bible says is right and wrong, then look at our lives and say, "Jesus is Lord." This gives us faith to look at all the weak areas of our lives and say, "He has already conquered them all on Calvary. As I let Him apply the power of the cross in daily prayer and meditation, in constant reference to the scriptures, seeking to meditate and to understand the will of God, He charges me with power and delivers me from carnal self. I carry my cross daily, not to crucify myself, but to yield to the crucified One."

What do these seducers say in the church today? They say that it doesn't matter if you don't practice righteousness, just as long as you confess that Jesus is Lord. Jesus said there would come a day when you would say, "Lord, Lord," and He would say, "Depart from Me, ye that work iniquity" (Matt. 7:23 KJV). You do the works of the devil; he that is righteous does the works of God. He that does the works of sin is under the influence of the devil, but thank God that there is hope for victory in the message of the Gospel. The hope is in the Word. You put the Word between you and the devil. The hope is the blood. When you put the Word and the blood between you and the devil, the anointing will break the yoke of the flesh. How often should we use the blood? The scripture says in 1 John 2:1, "And if any man sin, we have an advocate with the Father..." An advocate is one who stands between us and destruction. 1 John 1:9 says, "If we confess our sins, He is faithful and just to forgive us our sins and to cleanse us from all unrighteousness." So, every time sin appears – use the blood.

You and I must not allow ourselves to be seduced into believing that sin cannot be defeated. You and I must not allow ourselves to believe the big lie that it is impossible for Christians to live a sin free life. You can stay completely free of sin, even if you have to go to God every minute to get a fresh cleansing. The more you practice going to God for cleansing, the weaker sin's sway will be over you. At first there is a big battle because the devil thinks you don't know the truth. He thinks you are not committed to the truth. He thinks that if you don't start flying away to glory land after two or three weeks of trying the truth, you will just crash and give in. But once he finds out that you are committed to the Biblical order of Christian living, he will leave you alone. It makes perfect sense that if we are saved from the judgment and the presence of sin, we can also be saved from the practice of sin. There is victory over lust, alcohol, homosexuality, and lying. There is also victory over deceiving ourselves. There is real, joyous, triumphant victory when we stop playing games and quit worrying about stepping on someone's toes and just tell it like it is. I am not interested in games and parties. I am not interested in television, or in radio, or on the internet, or in Hollywood movie personalities. I am interested in the Holy Spirit, who wrote the book. I am interested in the Word , and I am committed to preaching it. I am interested in the Jesus who was incarnated in the womb of Mary and who came forth and lived thirty-three years without sin. In His thirty-three years, He conquered every carnal thing He faced in His life as a child, His life as a teenager, His life as a young adult... The same things we face. At the age of thirty, He stepped forth and a voice (A Lion's roar) came from Heaven saying, "This is my beloved Son, in whom I am well pleased" (Matt. 3:17). Then the Holy Spirit descended upon Him as a dove, anointing Him with the Holy Spirit and power. He began to expand this anointing and this blessing from person to person until, in time, the whole world was turned upside down; not by a persuasion of religion, but by the manifestation of the power of the anointing over sin in the flesh. Jesus, the Lion King, was anointed by the power of the Spirit to roar over all flesh, sin, sickness, and Satan and defeated them openly!

"For this purpose the Son of God was manifested, that He might destroy the works of the devil. Whoever has been born of God does not sin, for His seed remains in him; and he cannot sin, because he has been born of God" (I John 3:8-9). I am not asking you if you think you can live the rest of your life without ever having another temper tantrum, or being tormented with self-pity again. I don't even think I could do that, but I know Christ can. I know that if I daily take up my cross, if I daily seek for the bread of heaven, if I daily identify with His broken body and His shed blood, His life, manifested in my flesh, will bring me to higher and higher places of glory and victory.

THE ANTI-ANOINTING

"For we preach not ourselves, but Christ Jesus the Lord; and ourselves your servants for Jesus' sake. For God, who commanded the light to shine out of darkness, hath shined in our hearts, to give the light of the knowledge of the glory of God in the face of Jesus Christ" (2 Cor. 4:5-6). This is the glory of God, to say to humanity, "I give you victory. I give you victory over every body related problem from sin to sickness to every hindrance and every possible problem." That is the story of Israel in the wilderness. A cloud covered them to comfort them. A fire covered them to keep them warm. Manna fell from heaven to feed them. God said, "I am giving you victory over every need of the body." Christianity has been loaded down with fleshly, bodily, soulish, carnal things. We have become so occupied with how much I hurt, where I hurt, when I got hurt, and by whom I got hurt that we have forgotten that Jesus Christ was hurt until no beauty could be seen in Him. No man, no mortal, was so disfigured by the hurts of sin and by the destructions of sin, disease and death than Jesus Christ. He took it all. Now when we look at His face, we don't see the distortion, the disfigurement, the hurt and the pain. We see the Glorified One; He conquered it all. Every believer has Jesus Christ living within him or her. He is the treasure within us. Many people do not understand how He can live within them. I don't understand it either, so I never try to explain it; I just keep declaring it. Christ is living inside me. He has come into my flesh for the purpose of subduing everything that has to do with the carnal nature and sin.

"But we have this treasure in earthen vessels, that the excellency of the power may be of God, and not of us" (2 Cor. 4:7). God's power, the Holy Spirit that regenerated us and is forming the Christ likeness in us, is working in us mightily. He takes the most unlikely situation, a human being full of many sinful, natural traits, and says, "I am going to take all that and refashion and

199

reshape it." People are going to look into your eyes and see Jesus. They are going to watch your conduct and say, "Only someone in whom God has done something wonderful could go through those kinds of trials and still be nice and pleasant." Why is such power vested in such weak vessels? The same question can be asked concerning the treasure, which is so great that it seems to be out of place. Why is this power there? What is the treasure there for? The answer: The power is the treasure, and it is deposited in us so that God might get all the glory. We are hard pressed on every side, yet not crushed. We are perplexed, but not in despair. All the hurts, despair, and trials are the settings in which Christ reveals Himself in your flesh. When you are crushed, you don't glow. The crushing is to cause the place where you are hurting to become a place for His glowing.

2 Corinthians 4:8-10 KJV, "We are troubled on every side, yet not distressed; we are perplexed, but not in despair; persecuted, but not forsaken; cast down, but not destroyed; Always bearing about in the body the dying of the Lord Jesus, that the life also of Jesus might be made manifest in our body." Our problem is that we must identify with Him in His death in our body. You and I have a body; it is this body that must identify with His death. His death consisted of crushing, rejection, in getting knocked down, and in being pressured and tested. This identification with His death always shows up in physical, carnal, natural reactions. What is the purpose for this? The purpose is that the life of Jesus may be manifested in our bodies. Why is death in our bodies? So that life may also be there. We try to get rid of the dying so we can glow, yet it is through the dying that we glow. So nothing is ever going to go right in your life again until Christ shines forth brighter than your wants, brighter than your plans, and brighter than your timings. For example, when I was about seventeen years old, I was in a church service and had a Holy

Spirit experience. I stood up and said, "I have the power; get out of my way, devil." By three o'clock Sunday afternoon, that old devil was standing on top of me like a roaring lion seeking to devour me saying, "Where is your great faith confession now?" But when he got me down, the Lord rose up in me, and the Spirit began to work in me and renew me and showed me that when I'm down, I'm not really down. I'm just getting ready to get up again, and when I am up, I am able to roar in the anointing. The roar of His anointing far surpasses the roar of the devouring devil, and he scatters. He begins to avoid me because of my repetitious confessing (roaring). In time, when you have repeated your confession often enough, the word you are claiming will come to pass, giving you the dominion. Every Christian has a dominion even if it is only two feet wide, but once you begin to establish who you are in Jesus Christ that dominion will continue to grow and that devil will stay out of your way, that the life of Jesus may be manifested in your mortal body.

You may say, "I have been hit by one trial or another every day for the past two years." But I say you are still here; Praise God for that! When you get hit hard, and you feel bruised and crushed, and the old flesh says, "Where was God when I needed Him most?" God, inside of you, says, "I am right here with you. When you are in darkness, I am your light. When you are offended, I am your peace. When you are wounded, I am your healing. Now, let Me lift you a little higher than you have ever been before." Romans 8:11 KJV: "But if the Spirit of him that raised up Jesus from the dead dwell in you, he that raised up Christ from the dead shall also quicken your mortal bodies by His Spirit that dwelleth in you." If the same Spirit that raised up that mangled body from the dead dwells in you, He will also give life to your mortal body. Cancer will go. Liver problems will go. Asthma will go. Twisted backs will become straight. Romans

8:12-14 KJV: "Therefore, brethren, we are debtors, not to the flesh, to live after the flesh. For if ye live after the flesh, ye shall die: but if ye through the Spirit do mortify the deeds of the body, ye shall live. For as many as are led by the Spirit of God, they are the sons of God." This literally says, "Everyone who is born again has an anointing from the Almighty, through which He is working mightily in our lives".

Learning The Discipline of Spiritual Obedience

Learning the disciplines of spiritual obedience pays rewards today, tomorrow and forever. The longer we push it off, the fewer the rewards that can be received and laid up in this life. Absalom, David's treasured son, was just plain discontented. Most believers are discontented with their Christian status. They will say, "I am bored and disgusted with my Christian life. It must be the pastor's fault. He should learn a new style of preaching, or prophesy and pray over people more, or run around and jump up and down or do something different." I used to jump up and down and run around, and pray and prophesy over people every week, but I discovered that all I was doing was exhausting myself and just entertaining people. Now I try to just inform people and point them in the right direction, through prayer, and encourage them to take up their cross and follow Christ in a life of self-denial and obedience, where the Holy Spirit can begin to manifest and create a new dimension; the dimension of the Spirit-led life where the Christ-life is manifested and we are no longer bored. In the case of Absalom, he just wanted things to go his way. When things are not going my way in my spiritual life, I can be discontented, upset, on edge, fixing blame and trying to arrange things the way I want. This, of course, can lead into a works system where we start criticizing and judging others and trying to earn blessings instead of growing in faith and grace.

THE ANTI-ANOINTING

For years, I thought things should be happening in our local church the same way they happened in the book of Acts, and of course, they weren't, so I looked around to see who was at fault. I decided well; it must be the elders and the deacons; I thought I could see the rebellious demons in their eyes. When I realized that wasn't the case I decided the assistant pastors were at fault because they didn't have the boldness or knowledge to properly exercise their authority. When I realized that wasn't true (but some of them were exercising more authority than I was in some areas) I thought then it just had to be my wife. She needed to help me preach and teach more and be a better role model as "the pastor's wife" to the congregation. I have learned that none of us have anything except what is given to us by God. Jesus had only what the Father gave Him, and the Father didn't give Him some things until He was ready. He wasn't willing to give Jesus some things until he was thirty years old.

Discontentment about things not going the way we think they should open us up to a driving force where we become malicious elements in the body of Christ. We gripe about other people's weaknesses and murmur about how long it takes God to change the other party instead of getting into the prayer room, humbling ourselves, and seeking God's face. Aaron and Miriam had the problem of comparing themselves to others. Sometimes people compare themselves to their pastors, or other leaders, failing to realize that these men and women of God are only doing what God has anointed them to do. Stop comparing yourself one to another and saying, "Other people do things that are wrong and get away with it. Every time I do something wrong, I get into serious trouble." Stop comparing; because when you do, you open yourself up to the deception of unrighteousness as the scripture says, "for this reason God will give them over to strong delusion that they should believe a lie." (2 Thess. 2:11)

When a church splits, you can be assured that most of the people involved in the split have been given over to delusion to believe a lie – the lie that it is right to do wrong. You can also be assured when you see families torn apart by alcohol that someone has been deceived into believing that being an alcoholic is all right. Korah's problem in the Bible was that he wanted equality. Flesh always wants equality with Spirit. It wants as much time to do its pleasures as the Spirit does to do His pleasures. Let's give ourselves a little test. How much of our time do we give to edifying the spirit man compared to the time we give to edifying and taking care of the natural man? How do we measure up? The idea that equality is having the same opportunities is not the truth at all. Equality is having the same attitude of openness toward God. If Korah hadn't sought for equality, he could have come all the way through the wilderness wanderings, and gone into the Promised Land with everyone else. The spirit nature in us must teach the outer nature to be still. The carnal mind says, "How long are you going to take it? Stand up and tell them where they are wrong!" The spirit nature says, "Keep rolling your burden off on the Lord, until the Lord resolves the situation."

Is there an evil anointing? Yes, there is. Does it drive people until they say, "I'm going to straighten this thing out one way or the other, so help me God, even if everything gets wrecked in the process?" Yes, it does. Is there an evil anointing that takes hold of people and makes them feel good, right, and spiritual about doing the very things the Word says are wrong – the things that are destructive? Yes, there is. What do you do when you find these things coming into your life? You fall on your face and say, "God; I am only a human being, and I know my frame is frail and weak. I need your help, and I'm not getting up from here until You touch me." God can touch us; He can make us stable.

He can settle us and make us a light, a witness, and a testimony until sin has no place in us. The Bible's ultimate vision for our lives is that there not be sin mentioned among us.

1 John 3:7 KJV: "Little children, let no man deceive you: he that doeth righteousness is righteous, even as he (Christ) is righteous." (The area of deception is in the next sentence.) He that committeth sin is of the devil; for the devil sinneth from the beginning. For this purpose the Son of God was manifested, that he might destroy the works of the devil." What are the works of the devil? Practicing sin. The scripture says, "Whosoever is born of God doth not commit sin..." (1 John 3:9 KJV). In the Greek, this means that one who is born of God cannot practice sin. One who is committing sin, practicing sin, without conviction, has slipped into an area of deception. That person may be saying, "Everything is alright. My life is right; I know I am born again." But if one is practicing sin and there is no conviction, something is wrong. Deception is at work. If you practice righteousness, it is because Christ is working in you and has made His righteous nature available for you to let your members manifest His righteous nature. Where is Christ to be manifested? Is He to be manifested in a cloud in the middle of the church? No, that is an ethereal type or mental picture of God's glory. Christ is to be manifested in us. To whom is the manifestation of the Spirit given? It is given to every believer, and where is it to be manifested? Within His temple. What is His temple? Our bodies are the temple of the Holy Spirit. (see 1 Cor. 6:19)

Incorrect thinking, attitudes, and manners of conduct that are clearly contrary to sound doctrine are polluting Christianity. Works of the flesh are always contrary to sound doctrine. Jesus was manifested in the flesh to defeat sin, to conquer the carnal nature, to overthrow the Adamic influence and all the forces that lead us away from God and from that which is righteous. Everything that tells me Jesus was manifested in the flesh to take away the power of sin over the human race comes straight from the Gospel. Those who hear this are of God. Those who do not hear, John said, are not of God and they go out from among us because they are not of us. They are not of the mind to be fully for the Christ to take over the flesh, and to be "no more I that live but Christ that lives." The 'I' of the self-life must be totally crucified with Jesus Christ. As soon as a person is born again, he or she is filled with a drive to be like Jesus, and immediately starts trying to know what is right and wrong and to do what is right as much as possible.

Chapter 12
The Samson Anointing

The story of Samson is a mirrored microcosm of our time. He was given strength, wisdom, and a consecrated heart that allowed God to entrust into his hands a new beginning for his people. The prophets of old foretold the blessing that would come to all nations through the anointed seed of Abraham. Daniel captured the spirit of Samson's experience when he declared, "In the last days knowledge will increase." [especially the knowledge of God], and promised "but the people who know their God shall be strong, and carry out great exploits." (Dan. 11:32)

The Apostle Paul said that the finality of all his teaching is to be strong in the Lord. He declared that Jesus is the Anointed One, and said that if your strength is from any other source, it will fail you in trying times (see Eph. 6). Jeremiah said, "Thus saith the Lord, 'Cursed be the man that trusteth in man, and maketh flesh his arm, and whose heart departeth from the Lord. For he shall be like the heath in the desert, and shall not see when good cometh: but shall inhabit the parched places in the wilderness, in a salt land and not be inhabited. Blessed is the man that trusteth in the Lord and whose hope the Lord is. For he shall be as a tree planted by the waters, and that spreadeth out her roots by the river, and shall not see when heat cometh, but her leaf shall be green; and shall not be careful in the year of drought, neither shall cease from yielding fruit'." (Jer. 17:5-8 KJV)

Samson was truly a man of exploits. When Daniel said, "Do exploits," he used a phrase encompassing the totality of doing, in contrast to doing nothing. The phrase literally means, "Do everything that can be accomplished by knowledge and faith." The strength of the anointing is affirmed in Philippians 4:13: "I can do all things through the strength that flows from the Anointed One." Samson is called the strongest man who ever lived. What an example! He used his strength always and only to bring glory to God and to deliver his people. Compared to the job Samson was ordained to fulfill, he was weak and overshadowed by the immensity of the Philistine army. Through the strength of God, he was able to do magnificent and powerful exploits. We remember Samson as a solitary man, with no generals, troops, horses or chariots who single-handedly defeated armies of thousands. His example illustrates that we need not fear even great numbers of problems, because the anointing breaks every yoke and every burden. Paul not only said, "Finally, my brethren, be strong in the Lord, and in the power of His might," he also said, "Put on the whole armor of God, that ye may be able to stand against the wiles of the devil" (see Eph. 6:10-11). Our emphasis is not on the wiles of the devil, but on the protection provided by God's strength.

Each piece of armor makes us stronger:
1. From the helmet of salvation – a free gift
2. To the breastplate of righteousness – a free gift
3. To the shoes of the gospel of peace – a free gift
4. To the sword of the Spirit, the all powerful Word of truth – a free gift

The strength of the anointing stands as our protection. Those who know their protection have no fear. They know how to release the power of the anointing in absolute triumph and victory over every foe.

Consecration To God Means Denial Of Self

Consecration is symbolized by Samson's long hair; commitment is symbolized by his vow. His source of power was wisdom to first apply the spiritual to his own life. Samson's love for God and His people contributed to the strength of the truth that held him fast. Jesus put it this way, "If ye love Me, keep My commandments" (John 14:15 KJV). If you love someone, you will be committed to them, and out of that commitment will come consecration. If you love your job, you will be consecrated to it. When it is time to be there, you will be there, and when it is time to leave, you may stay a little longer if the job isn't done. Few people are as consecrated to God as Samson. Few are as committed to the local church as the apostles, but those who are hold fast by a lasting cord of strength. Many people are blown about in their Christian life because they have no cord of strength to hold them. We must be securely bound to the horn of the altar (see Psalm 118:27). How can we be bound to the horn of the altar? By consecrating every area of our lives to the Lord and His purposes. Samson could see that Israel had no natural strength to defeat the Philistines who continually molested their land. Samson was able to consecrate everything to God because he had no other source.

Samson realized God is the author and provider of everything, so he surrendered everything and, in essence, he said, "All that I am and all that I dream about I yield to God on the altar; I surrender my life." People often say that is a sacrifice to consecrate everything to God. I have come to believe that consecrating everything to God is more than a sacrifice; it is a privilege. To give your life to God is no sacrifice. To be informed, at any age of your life, that there is a power, a spiritual anointing that you can draw from, is the greatest privilege in the world. If you take your hands off your life and give everything to God, and say to Him – "My life is in Your life, Lord; my joy is in Your joy, Lord; my peace is in serving You, not in serving myself" – I guarantee you that you will find strength in the areas where before you have only known weakness. The longer I live, the more I realize that God turns my trials into triumphs, my mistakes into miracles, my mess into messages, and my sorrows into gladness.

Consecration means we learn God's ways. God's ways are not our ways; His thoughts are not our thoughts. His ways and thoughts are as high above ours as the heavens are above the earth. To learn God's ways and thoughts, we must first make a decision to do so. This decision must be made before we can experience consecration. Without consecration and the power it brings, you will never have the spiritual strength necessary to face life's battles or to obey God's commission in your life. Consecration begins by learning God's ways. God began to speak to me about learning His ways when I received the baptism of the Holy Spirit at the age of seventeen. What He told me had nothing to do with being a great pastor or apostolic prophetic leader, or even about living a moral life. The first thing God spoke to me then was "Learn My ways." Then He said, "Honor your father and your mother." My reply to Him was, "I do honor my father and mother." He said, "No, you don't; you find fault with your mother for leaving your birth father and remarrying and forcing you to love a step-father. You have already made up your mind that you are not going to be like them in some things. You have already started separating yourself and setting up walls and defenses. You have already made up your mind that you are going to be your own man and that you are going to run your life your own way, and I have told you to honor your father and mother." Now, don't mistake what I am saying. God does create every individual uniquely and distinctly different than every other person. The point is this- we should not belittle our parents and despise our families, rather, we should discover how God's light coming into our lives will bring the good, and the sweet, and the blessings from our families so that we are not a disgrace or a force of evil. Sooner or later, everyone will realize some of the good things that came from good family traits in their natural (or step) father's and mother's lives. Some people react with anger while others react with fear. Some people get their strength by getting their own way. They don't get angry; they pout. They act nice, but their niceness is a cover-up for their pouting. The Holy Spirit told me, "I want you to learn My way. I don't pout, I have joy; I don't go into anger, rage, or depression, I have victory." I said, "Fine, give me some; I'd love to have it. I'll trade in this junk for victory any day." He said, "All right, you are going to take it by faith. The fact is, son; you already have victory." I said, "I don't have it; if I had it, I could feel it." He said, "You don't feel it first. You believe it first." That's where the Holy Spirit and I parted company for a few days. Why? Because back then I couldn't believe anything that I couldn't feel or see, and I was that way for a very long time.

Samson had to learn the ways of God in order to fight against the lion and return to find its carcass full of honey. He had to learn that He was victorious before he saw the lion slain. You do too. You have to learn that the bitter is turned to sweetness before you see the honey in the honeycomb. Samson's long hair symbolized his consecration; it represented his yielding to the Spirit to not only know about God's ways, but also to walk in them. Picture Samson out in the wilderness; he's thirsty and has no water. He finds an old jawbone of a donkey and hears the Spirit of God say,

"There's water in it." You and I would probably say, "Sure there is, and there's also maggots in it, and there's probably even a snake curled up in it." But God told Samson to drink, and he did, and he was satisfied. Then God said, "This jawbone is stronger and more powerful in war than ten thousand swords of the Philistines. Take it and use it to defeat them."

Two things were required of Samson here:
1. He had to believe the Spirit.
2. He had to yield to the Spirit.

The same two things are required of us because only the Holy Spirit can empower us to walk out against all natural law and invoke a supernatural law, and to do it week in and week out without making an absolute mess of our lives. We see that the first step is consecration, which includes giving everything to God. Sooner or later, you will have your opportunity to give everything to God. It may be because you hear the call, or it may be because you have lost everything, but no matter which way it happens, when you give everything to Him, new strength will come into your life. This then is the key: give up your own ways, learn God's ways, then yield to His Spirit.

Samson's Vow
Samson's vow was never to partake of strong drink. That would be a great vow just because we know that strong drink alters, numbs, and nullifies the full strength and power of the human brain. Anything that robs us of mind power is a work of the devil. We need a sound mind, not a stupefied mind.

There are many things besides alcohol that dull the mind and spiritual life:
1. Getting angry.

2. Developing lustful impulses in the mind and the appetites (eating too much food can dull the mind, but fasting can illuminate it).
3. Gossip (it dulls the mind and spirit).
4. Technology, phones, electronic devices, television and video games (the one eyed demon) can dull, numb, and even pollute the mind (especially of our children and teenagers).

We need to cut off those things that can dull and pollute us. If there are things which are zapping your emotional and spiritual strength, let the Holy Spirit tell you what they are. Once He tells you what they are, it is up to you to cut them off.

Samson's Nazarite vow also represents separation from the world, the flesh and the devil. Many people, today, have little power compared to what the Church of Jesus Christ had in other days, which enabled it to alter the course of society from nation to nation. That power will return. Hundreds of thousands will make their way to God's altar; they will make a Nazarite vow to walk separate from the world, and it is not so much a matter of whether or not we personally sin in these things. It is much more that; it is a matter of whether or not we support the world system. So often, we do not even think about some of the things we do; we just do them. Some Christians have the attitude: "I'm saved by grace and it doesn't matter what I do." But it does matter. Grace teaches us to deny ungodliness and worldly lusts and to live soberly. We are to use wisdom and check things out, consider the cause and effect, and consider what we are going to do. Paul went so far as to say that if eating meat would cause another brother to stumble, he would not eat meat. We are to separate ourselves to a life of edification. Whether it be the way the church is run, or the way the home is run, the way the office is run, or the way society is run, we will not get into political debates to the point that we have division in the body of Christ – Christian against Christian. We will not get into debates over music to the point where we have hard feelings toward one another. That's what the world system does; if they don't like it, they fight over it. If the Christian is troubled by something, he surrenders to God and says, "Teach me what I am to learn, mold me and fashion me through this, the way I am to be changed. Lord teach me what to think, teach me what to say, teach me to be a minister of peace, kindness and love."

Samson's Wisdom

Samson had the wisdom to apply his strength in every place the enemy attacked him. One strength God has given all His people is the strength that comes from praying in the Spirit. Many people only speak in tongues to God while praising in church when they could speak in tongues over every place the enemy is attacking, and in the Spirit speak mysteries that would send the devil running. Samson applied his strength against the lion one way, but the way in which he applied his strength against the enemies was entirely different. He went out and caught a bunch of foxes, tied firebrands to their tails, and turned them loose in the enemy's fields and burned them down. The enemies at that time were the Philistines (who represent sin in our lives and the works of the flesh). Do you have a field of flesh that is about to bring forth a harvest of destruction? If you do, apply your strength, God says that you can burn it up. Turn the foxes loose – the little foxes that spoil the vine (see Song of Songs 2:15). These foxes are little things, little thoughts, little attitudes that we pet. They are foxes that we feed that we play around with. They are little foxes that say, "There's nothing so bad about this." For example: "A little internet pornography doesn't hurt anybody." "A little stealing of office supplies here and there won't hurt the company's profitability." That type of attitude is a little fox. Samson had the strength to turn the thing around and say, "Alright enemy, you're going to try to get me this way. I'll tell you what I'm going to do; I'm not only going to shut it out of my life, I'm going to go to work helping other people shut it out of their lives, and I'm going to set the tails on fire. Someday you may realize there is a little fox running around in your life called gossip, and you will say in your heart, "This is the end, I'm setting fire to the tail of this gossip thing, and every time I hear gossip, I'm going to say, 'Wait a minute, let's stop and pray for that situation and see how the Holy Spirit might minister to that need." May God give us the wisdom to apply our strength in every area the enemy comes against us.

Samson was locked up behind the gates of the city. Maybe you are in a situation where you are shut in financially, or maybe you have problems in your marriage. The devil is saying, "I've got you in my grip, you're going to miss all the joy, and all the activities. You're left with nothing; you don't have much in life." One day, you will rise up and say, "These problems are like cities with gates, and I'm going to take the gates off the hinges of every one of them." The Bible says Samson took the gates and pillars and threw them over the mountainside. The devil has told me many times, "You are captured in my city; you will be here the rest of your life." *Clank*! The gates went shut. *Clank*! The padlock was locked, and the demon guards stood in front of the gates and said, "This is your future." But I have the wisdom to take the strength of my consecration and my separation and pick up the promises of God and start focusing them against these gates and say, "I'm not living in this place. That's all there is to it, passion will not hold me, greed will not hold me; sickness will not hold me, and handicaps will not hold me!" Over the years, I have said to one walled city or another in my life or mind; "You are not my prison house. You are my next attack point." Those who crossed Jordan with Joshua said, "The walls will come down, and the enemies will be defeated. We shall triumph in every place the soles of our feet shall tread."

Finally, at the end of Samson's life, he was brought into the temple – the very seat of heathen worship. He stood there, after losing his eyesight, illustrating that it's not the viewpoint of the natural eyes that counts. It is the consecration (the separation) and the wisdom to apply the Holy Spirit anointing to each and every place the enemy strikes. There Samson stood, without physical eyes to lust for, or run after the pleasures of this world. Samson had only one thing left in his life. He knew to do the will of God, to apply his strength where he was. So he reached out, put his arm around those great pillars, and brought them down. The Bible says that in his death Samson defeated more enemies than he did his whole life. The lesson is that death-to-self brings down more enemies than our anointed self, running around and doing its own thing. Many Christians are failing because they do not have the strength to stand. They do not have the strength of Samson's consecration, his vow, and his wisdom. Because they have failed to move on with God and grow in grace and wisdom, they just keep starting over instead of going on to 'perfection', which in the Greek means, "development, maturity, and the mastery."

Chapter 13
The Builder Anointing

I Samuel 16:13 KJV: "Then Samuel took the horn of oil, and anointed him [David] in the midst of his brethren: and the Spirit of the Lord came upon David from that day forward. So Samuel rose up, and went to Ramah."

Samuel took the horn of oil and anointed David to be king of Israel. Samuel poured out the anointing oil upon David in the midst of his brethren, and the Spirit of the Lord came upon him from that day forth. David, because of his life, his heart, and his attitude, was chosen by God to be set apart in a particular place in God's kingdom – a place from which he would accomplish God's purpose in his life. When God pours the oil on you, He sets you apart that His Spirit might come upon you every time you need divine help and the wisdom of the Holy Spirit. Then, there was Saul. The Spirit of the Lord had left Saul, and another spirit came to him; a disturbing spirit that troubled him. God allows two kinds of spirits to be in the world: good spirits and evil spirits. The evil spirits take over when people reject the Holy Spirit and will not walk out their calling and vision, and God's will for their lives. For example: you can be anointed with bad oil if you are involved in gossiping, griping, complaining, or sowing division. Even if you are chummy with someone who is heavily into any of these things they can rub it in on you. It takes quite a bit of Holy Spirit "fuller soap to work it out." (see Mal. 3:2)

217

"He that is not with Me is against Me, and he who does not gather with me scatter." (Luke 11:23)

It is amazing the things that Jesus is for that we might be against. Sometimes we find ourselves protesting against doing things that Jesus clearly says He wants us to do, saying, "Lord, I can't do it, or I'm not interested in doing it. Furthermore, I'm not going to listen to the pastor who talks about it; I might even find another church if that pastor keeps talking and preaching about it." Regardless of your circumstances, if you yield yourselves as an instrument to God, He will cause the Holy Spirit to keep coming on you, helping you, empowering you, and carrying you out of your self-life bondage and giving you liberty in Christ. If you resist the Holy Spirit, then you will yield your members to the forces of evil. There are only two powers that we can yield to. We can yield ourselves to God or we can yield ourselves to the unclean forces of this world.

The Bible says of Solomon that he did everything according to the design of his father, David. David had the design; Solomon was the builder, and that is a wonderful thing to understand. The Bible says of Elisha that he followed Elijah in all things. Elijah said, "If you follow me and you are there when my life is over, you will receive a double portion of my blessing" (see 2 Kin. 2:9). Elisha followed Elijah in everything. Following someone in everything is a big calling and carries with it a tremendous amount of responsibility but the Spirit of the Lord will come upon those who do follow Him in everything.

Sometimes you will look at a person or a particular group of people and say, "Why does the Spirit come on them all the time?" The reason why the Spirit comes upon them is because

218

they are following hard after the Lord. Then you look at other people and say, "Why are they always troubled and disturbed?" One text says that Saul walked around in his house prophesying evil. Who would want to prophesy evil on their own house? One who is disturbed, out of control, and not walking in the Spirit. Such a person is a destroyer, not a builder. Here is an important factor: You can build for a while – a few days, weeks, months – and then you can turn around and start destroying everything you have built. On the other hand, you can learn to quit turning back. When you see yourself going back and destroying the very things you have built, you must learn to throw yourself upon God, because He is always a help in the time of your need. Jesus said, "Go and do what I do." He said, "I am going to build My church and the gates of hell will never prevail against it." Thank God, He never turned back to destroy the things He built. The Apostle Paul said, "Do what I do, I am a builder, I do what Jesus did." Two thousand years later, the message is still the same. Most of us know enough problems about ourselves, our families, and people in our church, that the weight of them could sink a ship. Do you think it's any better or worse now than it was a hundred years ago? Don't you think it is probably just about like it has always been? If you were to go back and read the headlines of the newspapers a hundred years ago and compare them with the headlines of the newspapers today, you would see that they are very similar. It would be the same even if you went back two hundred years. Read the history books. Read the Bible stories all the way back to Samson and Delilah. Go back to Gideon and his fears, and back to the Garden of Eden, and you will find that humanity is the same in every place and in every age. God has to be a great big wonderful God to build a church and have human beings involved, and still plan on keeping it a glorious church without spot or blemish or any such thing. Only God could do that, and if we are to be builders like He is, we must yield to the Holy Spirit's anointing.

1 Corinthians 11:31 tells us that if we will judge ourselves, we will not be judged. Even when the Lord does find it necessary to judge us, it is that He might not have to condemn us with the world. Perhaps you feel as though God has recently judged you. If He has, He didn't do it to condemn you; He did it to adjust you. Those who build walls have an instrument called a 'plumb line.' The plumb line indicates to the builder whether or not the wall is straight. When a carpenter or a framer builds a wall and holds up his plumb line to it, his plumb line tells him if the wall is straight. If it is not straight, he takes a hammer and pushes the wall back before he fastens it down. That's what you call bringing the wall into judgment. Then he brings it back and forth until it's on perfect plumb. God says, "If you will judge yourself, (that is, take the Word and judge your attitudes, reactions, and desires) conduct, and adjust your life to be in touch with My will then I won't judge you, but if you don't judge yourself, I will, and when I do, I will move you around and straighten you up."

Isn't it a wonderful experience to be straightened up by God? He straightens out the dents that were made in you when the world, flesh, or the devil over-hammered on you, and He fills in the hole that was made in your wall. He says, "I will fix it and patch it, and when I am done refining it, you will never know that the wall had ever been damaged." We have a wonderful God, who is doing exceeding abundantly above all we can ask or think, and He is able to fix everything that is wrong with us, and ultimately present us blameless before the Father with exceedingly great joy. God sometimes sends apostolic and prophetic pastors to the pulpit with a plumb line. Why? So that you might have something to test yourself by other than, "How am I doing compared to how someone else is doing?" This plumb line allows you to test yourself by: "How am I doing compared to the Word?" Why does God give us a plumb line? So we won't be condemned (judged) with the world. The tempter – the devil that old serpent, that liar, that thief, that murderer comes around to draw us out into bad attitudes, negatives, and denials. Even Peter, after he had just sworn by the Holy Spirit, "Thou art the Christ," turned around and denied Jesus". But God gave Peter a second chance to rectify his mistake. Jesus looked at Peter with those eyes of the plumb line and Peter went out and wept bitterly, and he got his heart right, and on the Day of Pentecost, he rose up as a great lion in his pride and jungle – he was a leader among leaders.

Read Matthew 3:1-12. All Judea and Jerusalem came to hear the preaching of John the Baptist, and among them came the Pharisees and Sadducees who, unfortunately, happened to be hypocrites. These people were very religious; they were doing the right things but with the wrong motives. They were doing the right things outwardly with no inward change. They were appearing to be godly, but in practice, they were doing what Jesus later said were the works of the devil. Can this same thing happen in a church? Can it happen in a ministry? Can it happen in a home? Absolutely! We don't need someone yelling, screaming and poking fingers at us. What we need is a straight face-to-face, heart-to-heart talk about the fact that we become servants of whatever we yield our members to. There are evil spirits in this world that try to take over our thoughts and attitudes, and influence our decisions, so that we actually turn against the very thing God has blessed us with.

Matthew 3:10 KJV: "And now also the axe is laid unto the root of the trees: therefore every tree which bringeth not forth good fruit is hewn down, and cast into the fire." Jesus says, "I am going to cut off evil fruit, and I am going to cut down fruitless trees." You may feel that there is an area of your life that is fruitless. It is this very thought of being fruitless that the devil uses against you, but you must always remember that God says, 'I am going to cut off evil fruit, and I am going to do more than that." John said, "I indeed baptize with water unto repentance, but He who is coming after me is mightier than I, whose shoes I am not worthy to wear. He will baptize you with the Holy Spirit and fire."

In the O.T., the anointing (having oil dumped on you) was symbolic of being baptized with what the N.T. describes as being baptized with the Holy Spirit. For as soon as Jesus came up out of the water, heaven opened, and the Holy Spirit in the form of a dove came and sat upon Him. Then, on the Day of Pentecost, the Holy Spirit came down as cloven tongues of fire and sat upon those gathered in the upper room. So the anointing that Aaron received was the equivalent of the baptism of the Holy Spirit. The baptism of the Holy Spirit is given in order to deal with hypocrisy, with pretending to be a Christian, and putting up a front, without the reality of being one. People all over the kingdom are trying to be something outwardly that they are not inwardly, and the Lord said, "I am going to give you the Spirit in power in such a way that you will become inwardly what you could never be otherwise." Then notice what He does; the text says that He not only will baptize you with the Holy Spirit and fire, He also has the winnowing fan in His hand, and He will thoroughly purge His threshing floor and gather His wheat into the barn and He will burn the chaff with an unquenchable fire. The process is continually being worked out in our lives, and it is also being worked out in the local church. There are times when we would like to get everyone in the church lined up in their relationship, and then ship them off to heaven so they will stay where we put them, but we can't do that. We cannot take the chaff out of others. You can't take the chaff out of me, and I can't take it out of you. Only God can do it, and He is constantly in the process of doing so on an individual basis. Only God can remove the chaff, so there is no value at all to use backbiting, gossiping, griping, or throwing stones in trying to do it yourself. None of these things will help the process at all. Neither is there any need for me or anyone to try to force you into perfection. The power that will get the job done is the fire of the Holy Spirit, which is sent into this world to deal with the carnal appetite. If we are endeavoring to keep the unity of the Spirit in the bond of peace, we will allow the builder's anointing to flow in our lives. We can either be building and gathering or we can be scattering and destroying. In both cases, the two go together. If we scatter, we destroy, if we gather; we build. We are to gather and build; therefore, we must endeavor to keep the unity of the Spirit in the bond of peace. We could all probably say that there are some people whom we would just as soon not be in the bond of peace with, but God requires that we endeavor and work at keeping the unity of the Spirit. God will give us an anointing that will bring us together in the bond of peace.

Prophecies that say some churches are going to blow up, split, be destroyed, all come from a destructive anointing. In Ephesians, Paul said that children of wickedness are energized by the spirit of disobedience. If there are two or more who will start saying, "We're going to work together; we're going to stop the backbiting; we're going to stop reacting to the things we heard someone else say," then the holy anointing will function properly and destroy all the destructive elements. Have you ever sat in a circle and played the pass-it-on gossip game? Did you ever start the story and hear how it turned out in the end – after everyone had repeated the way they thought they heard it? It makes you never want to open your mouth in public on anything serious at all. I used to occasionally have a question-and-answer time; I would preach a while, then I would say, "Now, tell me what you want to know concerning what I preached." I finally quit doing that because it was so devastating to hear what people thought I said. What you hear and receive when I preach is between you and God. Whatever you think I said, may God make something good out of it. There is no use in my trying to think that everyone heard the same thing. Whatever you are hearing – if you will endeavor to keep the unity of the Spirit – the anointing of the Holy Spirit will flow through your life, and you will be a builder. One example of endeavoring to keep the unity of the Spirit and the bond of peace is when we are irritated by the voice or mannerisms of a speaker, yet we choose to listen anyway and smile through it all. Doing so makes you a builder. On the other hand, if you do not endeavor to keep the unity of the Spirit, the destroying anointing will have you going around in strife. The scripture says; "Let nothing be done through strife or vainglory." Every time I travel, if I feel strife in my soul, I say, "Wait a minute, I'm headed for trouble. Disturbing, tormenting spirits have me on the run, and nothing would make them happier than them being able to run me right off the cliff." We need to stop and say, "God, teach me to build toward unity and forgiveness through Your grace." When we do, the building anointing will then be able to build good relationships.

Do you have problems with brotherly love toward certain people? I do, on occasion. The destroying anointing causes dissimulation. The Word says, "Love without division." One year, during Pastors Appreciation month, I received a nice card with the biggest "I Love You" on it that I had ever seen, but I had a problem with the card because the people who sent it had only recently said some of the most hurtful things they could say about my wife and I and our leadership abilities, and then they had the gall to send me a leadership appreciation card that said, "I love you." That's dissimulation. I looked up the scripture about love with a pure heart fervently, without dissimulation (see 1 Pet. 1:22). I wanted to write down what I had discovered and send it to the people who had sent me the card (as it confirmed my not so pleasant emotions I now felt toward those people), but I knew it would only cause conflict and possibly a war. I also knew that if I talked about it from the pulpit while I was in the attitude I was in; I would be inviting more distressing feelings that are ministered to us by those demons that just love to make us feel miserable when we are doing the wrong thing. Demons are continually waiting for you to get into a bad attitude, and when you do, they can give you a hundred reasons why your life isn't worth living, and why you should just throw in the towel, forget everything good you are doing for Jesus in the ministry, and that your Christianity is just a bunch of fakery. Satan will do everything he can to get us in a bad mood to extinguish our light so that we become a desolate city. May God help us to repent and go to the Mercy Seat and say, "Lord, I have been living for self. I have been carrying negative thoughts and judgments toward these people." We might even consider going to those people you have been feeling this way about and say, "I was out of order, and I wanted to be 'right' and you to be 'wrong'. I wanted to feel justified for my actions and decisions, I didn't handle your rejection of me in the right way, I was in a bad mood, and ask you to forgive me." Let's be builders." I am not advocating that everyone needs get up and start confessing faults one to another. You shouldn't confess unless the Spirit tells you to confess. Do not confess to me, because I've already heard enough. Confess to Christ. That's what the Mercy Seat is for.

ANOINTED TO ROAR

The true Christian is a soul-winner who is like a roaring lion. When a soul winner purposes in his or her mind to go out and win souls, the anointing flows out of that person's life. The soul-winner is anointed to roar with the Lion's roar. Their supernatural anointed roar will be heard (the gospel message of salvation) in every corner of the world. All who will hear and respond to the sound of the anointed roar will be saved from destruction and will forever become a member of the Bride (the body of Christ) and have all access, rights, and privileges of the Lion's anointing. So, go out and shout it from the rooftops and mountaintops (roar as loud and as clear as you can), you are anointed to roar that Jesus, the Lion of Judah is King of Kings, and Lord of Lords! Amen. The Bible says that the heavens declare His righteousness, and all the peoples see His glory. (Ps. 97:6)

The wild, fierce beauty of creation is but a window that offers a glimpse of the God, who created us. We need to throw open this window and allow God's untamed, limitless beauty to awaken a heavenly awe within us. As we open our eyes to the wonder of His creation, it arouses a God-yearning. Our spirit will respond to what it sees. Creation declares, "There is more!" More than what you see. More than what you hear. There is more than mere human mortality. There is the Immortal Lion, who is seated on high." Jesus our Christ came as the Lamb slain before the foundations of the earth, but the book of Revelation also reveals him as the Lion: "But one of the elders said to me, "Do not weep. Behold, the Lion of the tribe of Judah, the Root of David, has prevailed to open the scroll and to loose its seven seals" (Rev. 5:5). He is both our Lion and our Lamb. I wonder could there be a combination of two more contrasting images? The Message version of this passaged says that this lion "can rip through the seven seals." John, the author of Revelation, wept because, after a search of all of heaven, earth, and even the underworld, not one was found worthy to tear open the seven seals and begin the progressive reveal. Then the elder nearest John encouraged him to look, for there was a revelation of a Lion in our Lamb. He alone is worthy and initiates this work of opening the seals (unsealing). A rip or tear is a violent release. I am immediately reminded of the thick curtain of separation in the temple as it was ripped or rent in two (see Mark 15:38). The tear began at the highest place and ended at the lowest. I love this, for our God is always tearing asunder that which would hinder or separate any of us from all of Him.

In the mysteriously divine book of Revelation, this act of unsealing the scrolls of heaven sets things in motion on earth. Even now I sense God longing to unseal and show a portion of Himself to and in every one of us. If not, why would He have written this dramatic end of our earth story if it did not contain a revelation for each of us? I believe we are invited again not to despair or to weep but to lift up our eyes, look, and truly see. Our earth echoes the revelations and wisdom of heaven. How amazing that our heavenly Father designed His creation to open our hearts. Each plant, animal, element, and landscape says, "Arise and be all you were created to be." Accordingly, God sets out the entire creation as a science classroom, using birds and beasts to teach wisdom. (Job 35:11)

The wonder of God's love and the extent to which He will go to impart His wisdom to us is almost too vast to grasp. We should not be surprised by this; He is, after all, the Creator, who declares: "For every beast of the forest is Mine, and the cattle on a thousand hills. I know all the birds of the mountains, and the wild beasts of the field are Mine. If I were hungry, I would not tell you; for the world is Mine, and all its fullness" (Ps. 50:10–12). In Proverbs we are charged, "You lazy fool, look at an ant.

Watch it closely; let it teach you a thing or two" (Prov. 6:6). I believe God is asking us to do something similar now. He is asking us to look at the lion and to learn. He invites us to look closely at the lion, watch him closely, and let Him awaken our untamed nature, our fierce beauty, and our unbridled strength so we (the church) can rise up and be the anointed courageous men and women (anointed lions) we have been called to be.

How does a lion show strength and courage in men and women? How can we rise up like the lion? Each of us will have our unique response, but this glimpse of a lion's characteristics (the anointing) gives you deeper insight. The Lion of all lions, Jesus, the Lion of the tribe of Judah, rises to gather strength in this last day. He rises to greet and groom other lions. He rises to hunt alongside other young lions. He rises to move the young to safety. He rises to confront enemies (the devil) that threaten His pride. He rises to ride the heavens and walk the earth as King. I have endeavored to write and teach about the lion as a picture of how every son and daughter of the Most High can embrace his or her strength, develop courage, defend, and affect change in his or her life. There is a lion hidden within you! You are anointed to roar! It is my prayer that, by the time you finish this book, you will have found answers to your deepest questions, and with those answer something fierce, beautiful, and wild will be awakened in you (your anointing!) Child of God, you are Anointed to Roar!